BEGINNER'S GUIDE TO STARTING A YOUTUBE CHANNEL: 2023 EDITION

How To Become a Social Media Influencer & Content Creator

By Ann Eckhart

TABLE OF CONTENTS

INTRODUCTION

CHAPTER ONE: CREATING YOUR YOUTUBE & ADSENSE ACCOUNTS

CHAPTER TWO: FILMING EQUIPMENT & SET-UP

CHAPTER THREE: FILMING TIPS

CHAPTER FOUR: YOUR CHANNEL'S THEME & CONTENT

CHAPTER FIVE: HOW TO EARN MONEY ON YOUTUBE

CHAPTER SIX: YOUTUBE ACCOUNTING MADE EASY

CHAPTER SEVEN: MARKETING & PROMOTION

CHAPTER EIGHT: BEST PRACTICES

CHAPTER NINE: A DAY IN THE LIFE

CONCLUSION

ABOUT THE AUTHOR

INTRODUCTION

Are you looking for a home-based business that allows you to be creative and make money? Or do you already have an established business but are looking for new ways to market it? Then starting a YouTube channel may be the answer!

For years, I have been teaching people how fun and easy it is to start a YouTube channel for both fun and profit. And in this, the 2023 edition of my Beginner's Guide to Starting a YouTube Channel, I walk you step-by-step through filming, editing, uploading, and promoting your videos.

YouTube can be a business on its own or a supplement to an existing business. There are online content creators who make a full-time living creating YouTube videos. And there are other businesses, both large and small, that use YouTube as another way to reach customers.

I began my YouTube journey over a decade ago. I was five years into running a home-based reselling business where I sold wholesale items on Ebay and Amazon. I'd just purchased a new home and was settling into my new workspace when my sales started to dip.

I had been early to the online selling game. When I first started selling on Ebay, Ebay was the only shopping site that allowed third-party sellers. In fact, Ebay was pretty much the only website that sold anything besides books. If you are old enough to remember, Amazon initially started as an online bookstore. It took them several years before they started to sell anything other than media.

For those of us who were the first to sell online, there was virtually no competition anywhere on the world wide web. Ebay was not just "the" place to sell; it was the "only" place to sell. Sales came in fast and steady with little effort other than getting a listing up and then shipping it out. My business was, I have to admit, pretty easy to run. I sold on Ebay exclusively for nearly two years before expanding to Amazon. I had phenomenal growth every year, and it seemed as if the possibilities were endless.

Until the year the floor fell out from under me. That was the year the rest of the retail community started to catch up, starting their own e-commerce websites and beginning to sell on Ebay and Amazon.

Not only were other people starting to sell the same items that I was, but the wholesale companies I bought from were also starting to sell directly to customers online, too. After years of no competition, I was suddenly surrounded by competitors who were undercutting my prices and offering perks I could not afford, such as free shipping. Seemingly overnight, I could no longer stay competitive, and my business seemed doomed.

But then I stumbled upon YouTube. And through YouTube, my business was given a new life. In fact, YouTube, specifically those creating YouTube videos, saved my business.

I had never watched a YouTube video before that fateful day when I did an internet search about selling on Ebay. I was hoping to find a book or website to help me figure out what to do with my business, a magic bullet to help me salvage what I had worked so hard to build. I was desperate but out of ideas of my own.

So, imagine my surprise when my search results revealed several YouTube videos with titles such as "What I sold on Ebay from garage sales" and "How I make money selling used clothing from thrift stores." Intrigued, I followed the links and found a small group of people who called themselves "pickers."

These "pickers," or "resellers," as most people now call them, were making videos on YouTube about their thriving Ebay businesses. And not one of them was buying new items wholesale the way I had been. While buying brand new items was easy for me to order and list, these sellers, who ran their businesses from their homes, were earning more money than I ever had sourcing secondhand items.

I quickly became immersed in the videos these "pickers" were sharing about how they were selling garage sales, and thrift store finds on Ebay. While I had always known that there were antique dealers on Ebay, I somehow never made the connection that I, too, could sell secondhand items online. I saw antiques as a specialized skill set, one I knew nothing about. But I soon learned that "antiques" were just the tip of the iceberg when it came to finding items to resell. And I quickly saw how I, too, could sell used items.

My business, which I had thought was over, suddenly got a new life as I learned all about reselling. While it was hard to give up the ease of ordering new items directly from the manufacturer (complete with photos and measurements), I was desperate to avoid returning to working for someone else. So, I hunkered down and learned all that I could.

It took a lot of trial and error, but I successfully transitioned my business from selling new gift products to selling thrifted finds. I started scouring estate sales for vintage collectibles and went to half-off day at the thrift store to buy clothing to resell. I gave up selling on Amazon and refocused my efforts on Ebay, liquidating my remaining wholesale inventory and listing everything from vintage collectibles to electronics.

This new business model saved my business, and it was thanks to the people in the "picking community" who were making videos on YouTube. Those YouTube creators and the YouTube site itself not only saved my business but learning how to resell secondhand items eventually led me to write books such as the one you are currently reading!

From having an online gift shop to reselling secondhand items to becoming a full-time author. It's been a wild two decades of self-employment! And in between those business adventures, I also started my own YouTube channel.

When I first started watching YouTube videos, I had no intention of starting my own channel. Rather, I interacted with the video creators by leaving comments on their uploads and formed friendships that last to this day. It was fun to talk to other Ebay sellers, and we happily shared information with one another, celebrating our successes and encouraging each other when things weren't going well.

However, they also all encouraged me to start my own YouTube channel. But I was terrified to upload my own videos. Not only did I hate public speaking and being on camera, but I also had no idea how to start a YouTube channel.

Eventually, though, I got up the courage and took the leap to start my own channel. With some help from my YouTube friends, I finally figured out how to film and upload videos.

And my first YouTube videos were terrible! I used an old iPhone (I think it was an iPhone 4), and since I initially filmed in my basement office, the lighting was terrible, which made my videos dark. I constantly forgot to look at the camera, and I had to remind myself to speak up to be heard. And don't even get me started on my camera angle. All in all, my videos were a mess.

I wanted to quit YouTube at that point. But with the encouragement of my "picking" friends, I kept going, slowly gaining confidence in my filming abilities. And I also started growing an audience.

I would gladly give you the URL to my first channel so you could see how bad my videos were, except that it no longer exists. Why? Well, back when I first started on YouTube, you could sign up for a channel using any email address, so I used the one that came with my internet provider. However, when Google introduced monetization, you could only monetize your channel if you signed up using a Gmail account, the email that Google provides.

I had built an audience on a channel I could not make money on. So, I had to start a brand-new channel using a Google account and began the long process of rebuilding my audience.

Don't worry: You will not have to face this same issue. Today the only way to start a YouTube channel is when you sign up with a Google Gmail account.

It took a while for me to move my audience from my old channel to my new one, but once I had, I deleted my original channel and focused on my new channel. Honestly, it was nice to start fresh as I was more comfortable on camera and had upped my production value. I'm also glad those old videos aren't around to haunt me (I told you they were bad, and I meant it!)

However, the best part of my new channel was that I was finally earning money from my videos with Google AdSense. There are many ways to earn money on YouTube, and the first is with Google AdSense. Google owns YouTube and sells advertising that runs before, during, and after videos. Google shares this advertising revenue with YouTube creators.

I didn't earn much money to start, maybe a couple of hundred dollars a month. But I loved making videos and being part of the YouTube "reselling community." For me, YouTube was fun. I was not only making friends, but I was learning so much about business. And the extra money was a nice bonus.

After a few years with just one channel, I started a second

channel. Why start a second channel when I already had a successful one? Well, it was because I wanted to upload different content. While my first channel focused solely on my Ebay business, I initially started my second channel to focus on my Walt Disney World vacation vlogs. At the time, I anticipated going down to Orlando, Florida, twice a year and filming lots of videos for that channel.

However, life happened, and I became a full-time caregiver for my elderly father. Not only were vacations out of the question, but full-time reselling had to take a backseat as it required too much time and effort. I needed to streamline all my businesses, and that included YouTube.

Figuring out what to do with my YouTube channels took me on a roller coaster of a journey with attempts at various content. I tried lifestyle vlogs and subscription box reviews; I even had a short-lived podcast-style show called "The Reselling Report." I felt like I was spinning in a million directions, trying to find something that worked. At one point, I almost gave up on YouTube.

But giving up YouTube was harder than sticking with it. After all, I had spent years growing my channels. Eventually, I had to take an "I can only do what I can do" attitude regarding what types of videos I could film and which channel to put them on. At the end of the day, I reminded myself that I had started making YouTube videos for fun. Sure, the extra money was nice. But I needed to enjoy myself if I was going to continue producing content.

Today, I still have my two YouTube channels. "Ann Eckhart" is my main channel, where I post single-topic side-down videos. And my second channel, which was once titled "SeeAnnAtWDW," is now "Ann Eckhart Vlogs," where I post, you guessed it, vlogs. I film shopping vlogs, day-in-the-life vlogs, and in 2022 added in vlogs of the new Lost Island Theme Park that opened in my city. I can't make it down to Orlando to film Disney vlogs, but I can drive to the theme park that is 10 minutes from my house and film videos there.

As I said earlier, my YouTube journey has been a roller coaster. There have been times when I was consistently earning over $1,200 a month from my videos and other times when I had to take a break from filming, which plummeted my earnings. I have changed my content and upload schedule more times than I can count, and my channels have suffered for it as YouTube favors consistency.

Today, however, I have found a happy medium for being a YouTuber. As I said, I now film what I can when I can. I still have a good group of friends I've made on YouTube, and I still love to watch other YouTube channels. YouTube is part of my daily routine, and I can't see that changing any time soon.

Fortunately for you, you will be learning from all my mistakes, which will help you succeed with your channel right out of the gate. From setting up your account and learning how to upload videos to building your brand and earning money, I'll be teaching you all of the ins and outs of YouTube.

This book may be titled *Beginner's Guide To Starting a YouTube Channel*, but in fact, it is the ultimate guide to help you not only start a channel but also grow it. With just a computer, camera, and internet access, anyone can start a YouTube channel. But it takes work and perseverance to grow a channel and earn money from it.

Whether you have yet to start your YouTube channel or have already started posting videos, I guarantee this book has something to help you succeed and grow!

CURRENT YOUTUBE STATISTICS

- 2.6 billion active monthly users
- 62% of global consumers use YouTube
- YouTube is the second most popular search engine after Google

- YouTube is available in over 100 countries
- YouTube videos are available in 80 languages
- Every day, people around the world watch 1 billion hours of YouTube videos
- 62% of businesses use YouTube
- 63% of YouTube watch time comes from mobile devices
- 90% of consumers say they discover new products on YouTube
- 500 hours of video is uploaded to YouTube every minute

CHAPTER ONE: CREATING YOUR YOUTUBE & ADSENSE ACCOUNTS

YouTube was founded nearly seventeen years ago by three PayPal employees: Chad Hurley, Steve Chen, and Jawed Karin. PayPal, if you remember, was Ebay's original payment processing system. How funny is it that the men who would start YouTube initially worked for PayPal, the payment service I used to run my Ebay business? It's a small tech world, indeed!

According to internet lore, Hurley, Chen, and Karin started YouTube in a small space above a Japanese restaurant and a pizzeria in San Mateo, California. It was Karin who was the star of the first video ever uploaded to YouTube: "Me at the Zoo." It was only a shaky 19-second-long clip, but it would revolutionize the internet space forever.

Hurley, Chen, and Karin activated the domain name "YouTube.com" on February 14, 2005, with the original concept of it being an online dating series. However, when that idea failed, the young entrepreneurs focused on making YouTube a place for non-computer experts to publish, upload, and stream videos through standard web browsers and household modems. Initially, video clips were limited to 100 megabytes with as little as 30 seconds of footage.

Everything changed a year later when Google purchased YouTube in 2006 for $1.65 billion in stock. After Google purchased YouTube, the site grew quickly, reaching 43% of the video market by the end of 2010. In the next few years, much was done to make YouTube more accessible to small content creators while also building the company up, including adding AdSense advertising payments for creators. Now people can upload videos not only for fun but also for profit.

Over the years, YouTube has grown from a small niche website to a platform with over two billion users worldwide. Today, creators, both large and small, produce videos for nearly two billion active users across the globe. And with nearly 122 million viewers logging onto the site every day, YouTube has shown no signs of slowing down, continuing to grow yearly.

Needless to say, YouTube has become a part of everyday life for a large population of people across the globe. With content ranging from cooking, crafting, traveling, and family vlogging to gaming, beauty, style, news, comedy, finance, and business, there is something for everyone to watch on YouTube. And there is always a ready audience of YouTube viewers searching for videos.

So, you may be wondering, is there a place for YOU on this overcrowded site? The answer is YES! Anyone can start a YouTube channel today and work to make it successful. The key is that you must start your channel, which you will learn how to do in this chapter.

I won't lie to you, however. YouTube is a much more competitive space than just a few years ago. New creators are continually joining the site, and videos' production value is lightyears ahead of where they were initially.

To build a successful and profitable channel, you need to be committed to filming good, consistent content. Fortunately, the actual process of filming and uploading videos is the easy part. It's the marketing, promotion, and management of a channel where creators do the real work.

YouTube makes it easy to upload videos, but it is Google that will pay you to do it. YouTube creators can make money on the site because Google owns the actual website itself. Google enabled channels to start making money from their videos in 2008. The rate they pay varies by the type of ads that run on the videos, but everyone is paid per 1,000 views. Some people make 50 cents per 1,000 views, while others earn hundreds.

Not only has this partnership between YouTube and Google been beneficial for channel creators, but it has also proved to be a lucrative opportunity for advertisers as they can reach customers across the globe for a fraction of the cost of television advertising. Think about it: Don't you see a lot of companies advertising on YouTube that you have never seen advertise on television? Google has given small companies a way to reach way more customers than if they were just running ads on TV.

However, it isn't just Google that will pay you to make videos. Brand sponsorships are another way creators can earn income on YouTube. Some creators actually earn more from sponsorships than they do AdSense! While most people, such as myself, look at YouTube as a way to bring in some additional income, while other people have made YouTube their full-time job.

YouTube currently runs ads on over a billion video views every week, giving a cut of the advertising revenue to creators. I will be talking in-depth about making money from your videos from AdSense, sponsorships, and other ways later in this book. But before you can make any money, you must properly set up your YouTube and Google accounts.

Since Google owns YouTube and controls the AdSense advertising that pays you for your videos, **you must first sign up with Google to create a YouTube channel** that will earn you ad revenue.

As I talked about in the *Introduction* to this book, when I started my first YouTube channel, I did not sign up through Google but instead registered through a different email account. Because I did not sign up for my first YouTube channel through a Google email address, that initial channel could not be monetized. Despite consistently uploading videos and building an audience, I never earned a penny from those videos.

Fortunately, you do not have to worry about making the same mistake I made because today, you can only get a YouTube channel through Google. You can skip this next section if you already have a Gmail account through Google. But if you do not have a Gmail email address, it is free and easy to set one up. Here is how:

GOOGLE ACCOUNT: To sign up for a Google account that will allow you to create a YouTube account and a YouTube channel, head to the Google Account sign-up page at **accounts.google.com/signup**. The registration process is quick, easy, and completely free.

The Google account page will allow you to create a **Google account**, a **YouTube account**, a **Google "@gmail.com" email address**, and a **YouTube channel**, all in one place.

Simply follow the online prompts to complete the process. A Google account will first give you your own *YouTube account*, which will enable you to interact with other creators' content (such as subscribing to channels, giving videos a "thumbs up" or a "thumbs down," and leaving comments). If you've been watching YouTube videos before this, you may have noticed the inability to leave comments on videos, as this is only available to those with a YouTube account.

In addition to giving, you your own *YouTube account,* Google will also then give you your own *YouTube channel.* However, it is up to you if you want to activate your channel.

Many people with YouTube accounts never create their channels, but the option is already built-in once you have an account. You will be prompted to create your channel by Google; the process is as simple as naming your channel. Do not worry if you are not ready to upload anything right away; the creation of your channel simply means that it is there if and when you are ready.

CHANNEL NAME: When you create your Google account, you will choose a username. Most people make this their actual name, and I recommend that. You can then choose a different name for your actual YouTube channel. Your Google username is different from your YouTube channel name.

Be sure to choose your YouTube channel name wisely. Google usually prompts you to make it the same as your account name, but you can select any name you like, just as long as another account is not currently using it. While you may just be starting on YouTube for fun now, you do not want to limit yourself from growing your brand in the future. Many established, successful YouTube channels have names unrelated to their content because the people behind them never anticipated how large their channels would grow.

And while you can change your channel name if you decide to later on, it can confuse your subscribers. I named my first YouTube channel, the one that is no longer active, the same as my Ebay store name, the name under which my reselling business was registered. Since I was then only creating Ebay content at the time, that name made sense.

However, I started a now-defunct blog called "SeeAnnSave," where I posted about couponing and free samples. It was at this same time that I started my second YouTube channel using a Google account so that I could earn AdSense on my videos. I

15

decided to delete my first channel and named my new YouTube channel "SeeAnnSave" to match my blog, as I wanted to post money-saving videos in addition to my reselling content. Most of my followers on YouTube today subscribed to my channel when it was "SeeAnnSave" and still call it that to this day.

However, I eventually closed my blog and changed my channel name to my name, "Ann Eckhart." Since I publish books under my own name, it made the most sense to "brand" all of my content under the same name, YouTube included. I also changed my social media handles to match. "SeeAnnSave" became "Ann Eckhart" on YouTube, Facebook, Twitter, and Instagram.

While Google allowed me to make the name change, I had to completely rebrand everything, including my channel name and channel artwork and logos. Plus, I had to change the names of all my social media accounts. It was a considerable undertaking, and while it was worth it in the long run, it took a lot of work. Plus, I had to continually explain to my subscribers why the name was different for quite a while. If I had to do it all over again, I would have stuck with naming my channel my own name the way it is now.

And as I mentioned, some people still see me as "SeeAnnSave." So, while you are not locked into the first name you choose, note that it is better to get it right the first time to save yourself the headache of changing everything later on. And if you cannot come up with anything unique, it is perfectly fine to use your real name. In fact, many YouTube creators who started with quirky channel names are now changing them to their real names.

Note that while you can change your YouTube channel name, you cannot change the URL for your channel yourself. The URL can only be changed by contacting Google directly.

My main channel URL still ends with *seeannsave*, and my second channel URL ends with *seeannatwdw*, as I initially started it as a Walt Disney World vacation vlog channel. While I changed my account names so that my primary channel NAME is now *Ann Eckhart,* and my second channel NAME is *Ann Eckhart Vlogs,* the URLs for both channels have not changed. It is confusing, I know!

To be honest, I still have not bothered to contact YouTube to ask about changing my URLs as, in the end, the website address itself does not matter too much. It is the name of the channel that I personally feel is important. Most viewers will either search for your channel name or just subscribe to your channel outright to find your videos; very few people will actually type in your channel's URL address, much less even know what it is. You can copy and paste your channel's URL to post it to your other social media accounts, allowing people to simply click on the link to be taken right to your channel. There is no need to type in the actual address. And if you don't like the look of your URL, you can use the tinyurl.com website to shorten it.

If you plan to make your YouTube channel your main website, you may want to purchase a dedicated URL from a site such as GoDaddy.com and have it directed to your channel. For instance, I own the URL AnnEckhart.com, which I have set to direct users to my Amazon Author Page automatically. My books are my primary source of income, and I want people to visit my author page above all of my other websites. However, I would point the URL directly to my channel if YouTube was my full-time job.

Owning the URLs to your channel name is a good idea in the long run. While you may start your channel just for fun, it may grow to the point where you want to "brand" your content. And if your Google AdSense grows significantly, you will want to direct people to your channel; that is much easier with a dedicated URL. Plus, you want to secure your URL name before someone else buys it.

URLs are inexpensive to obtain and are something you will want to investigate as your channel grows. Choosing the ".com" version is the most logical, but if your channel becomes large, you will want to secure all the domains (.org, .net, etc.). And if your channel name is different from your own name, you may want to own the URLs for your name, too. I still own the "SeeAnnSave" URLs, the URLs for my own legal name, the URLs for my Etsy shop and low-content books, and the URLs for pen names that I publish fiction books under.

SET UP YOUR ADSENSE ACCOUNT: While you used to start earning AdSense money right out of the gate on YouTube, in 2019, Google changed the requirements for becoming monetized (i.e., allowing you to place ads on your videos to earn a cut of the revenue from them). Now a channel needs to have 1,000 subscribers AND 4,000 hours of views before it can start making AdSense money. YouTube is now taking AdSense away from inactive channels and making creators re-earn their monetization by getting back up to 4,000 watch hours within a year.

While these new requirements are frustrating for new YouTube creators and also to YouTube creators who may have stepped away from their channels for a bit and lost their AdSense, you can get your channel to monetization standards rather quickly with dedication and consistency. I will go over ways to grow your channel later in this book. But first, more about AdSense.

According to Google, AdSense works in three steps:

1. You make your ad spaces available by pasting ad codes on your blog or website and placing ads on your YouTube videos.
2. The highest paying ads appear on your site as advertisers bid to show in your ad spaces in real-time auctions.
3. Creators are paid directly from Google, with Google handling the process of billing all advertisers for the ads that show up on your content.

As part of the AdSense Program, Google delivers ads to your blog, website, and/or YouTube channel via their Google Ads system.

Google then pays you for the advertisements displayed on your videos based on user clicks on ads OR ad impressions, depending on the ad type.

Creators cannot choose the ads that appear on their sites/videos. Advertisers tell Google the content they want their ads targeted on, not the other way around. Tech companies are willing to spend more on ads than, say, beauty products. And come election time, all bets are off as campaign ads flood the site. Despite your own political views, you cannot control if a candidate you don't support places ads on your videos.

Google uses three methods to determine which ads are placed; according to them, these are:

1. **Contextual Targeting:** Google technology uses factors such as keyword analysis, word frequency, font size, and the overall link structure of the internet to determine what a site or video is about and precisely how to match Google ads to that particular content.
2. **Placement Targeting:** Under this format, advertisers can choose specific ad placements to run their ads. Ads that are placement-targeted may not be precisely related to a page's content but are instead hand-selected by advertisers who have decided that there is a match between the products/services and what your readers/viewers are interested in.
3. **Personalized Targeting:** This offering enables advertisers to reach users based on their interests, demographics, types of websites they visit, the apps on their mobile devices, the cookies on their web browsers, the activity on their devices, previous interactions with other Google ads, and their own Google Account activity and information.

To monetize your videos, you will first need to become a **YouTube Partner**, which we will discuss in the next section of this chapter. As I mentioned, you now must have 1,000 subscribers and 4,000 hours of watch time before you can monetize your videos. However, if you have a blog or website, you will want to go ahead and sign up for a Google AdSense account now, as you can start earning money from ads on websites immediately. There is no threshold you need to meet to make money from Google ads on a website. I was earning Google AdSense on my blog a couple of months before I started making money on my videos.

Simply visit **google.com/adsense/start** to begin the application process. Note that you will need to go through a verification process to qualify for an account, including providing your **social security number** for tax purposes and your **bank routing information** for direct deposit of your earnings. Some people are wary of providing this information, but it is the same as you would do if you were applying for a job. If you expect Google to pay you, they will need your information for tax purposes. Google sends you a 1099 tax form if you make money from ads within a calendar year.

Note that Google may also send you a PIN code via mail or email that you will need to provide to complete the application process. The process changes every so often, but Google will provide you with all the instructions to follow when submitting your application.

You can choose to have your AdSense earnings mailed to you or sent via direct deposit to your bank account. You must reach $100 in total AdSense earnings across all platforms (blog/website/YouTube) to receive a monthly payout. For years, I had AdSense on both my blog and YouTube, so I easily met that $100 monthly threshold every month. If you don't meet the $100 payout minimum in a month, the amount will carry over into the following months until you reach $100. Once you earn the money, you can't lose it; you just may have to wait until they release it to you.

In late 2021, I shut my blog down and now only earn AdSense

through YouTube. However, I still earn enough AdSense between my two channels to receive a monthly payout, which is automatically deposited into my bank account around the third week of the month.

Since AdSense is income, you do have to pay taxes on the money you earn. Fortunately, Google makes it easy by sending users tax forms every year. You can have your Google 1099 form mailed to you, or you can download it from your account. Do not worry about missing it: Google will notify you when the forms are available. If you don't get a notification, you simply log into your Google AdSense account, and you will find your tax form there to print.

While AdSense is usually the most significant chunk of income for most channels, you must also keep track of any sponsorship or affiliate money you receive. Not all companies will send out tax forms for brand deals or affiliate advertising income. I have several affiliate marketing partnerships that never send out tax forms, but I still keep track of the money they pay me. I will discuss these additional forms of income and managing your YouTube finances later in this book.

Once you have completed the application process and have been approved for an AdSense account, you can begin placing AdSense ads on your blog or website. However, you will have to wait to be eligible to join the **YouTube Partner Program** to start monetizing your YouTube videos. You cannot join the program until you reach 1,000 subscribers and 4,000 watch hours. Your channel won't automatically be monetized when you reach these goals. Joining the YouTube Partner Program is an additional step you will need to complete; do not worry, as Google will prompt you to do it once your channel is eligible.

BECOMING A YOUTUBE PARTNER: After you have created your Google account, YouTube channel, and AdSense account, there is one more step you will need to take before you can start earning money on your videos, and that is to become a **YouTube**

Partner.

Once your channel reaches 1,000 subscribers and 4,000 watch hours, YouTube will prompt you to sign up with their YouTube Partner Program.

According to YouTube, *The YouTube Partner Program (YPP) gives creators greater access to YouTube resources and features,"* including access to YouTube's creator support teams, copyright match tools, and monetization features.

The minimum eligibility requirements to join the YouTube Partner Program include:

- Following all the current YouTube monetization policies (these are frequently updated; once you are going through the application process, you will be prompted to agree to them)
- Live in a country or region where the YPP is available
- Have 4,000 valid public watch hours within 12 months
- Have more than 1,000 subscribers
- Have a linked AdSense account (again, this is an excellent reason to create your AdSense account even before you are eligible to apply to be a YouTube Partner, as you will be ready to go once you meet the requirements)

Here is an abbreviate *YouTube Partner Program* application checklist:

1. Make sure your channel follows all policies and guidelines. You will go through a standard review process when you apply to check if your channel meets these standards.
2. Enable 2-Step Verification for your Google account, which means you will protect your account with both your password and an additional device.
3. Have at least 1,000 subscribers and 4,000 valid watch hours on your channel.

4. Sign YTP terms to be notified when you are eligible to apply to become a YouTube Partner. You can do this manually, although YouTube will prompt you once you meet the subscriber and view thresholds.
5. Make sure you only have ONE AdSense account (you cannot have multiple accounts under your name).
6. Once you sign the YouTube Partner Program terms and connect your AdSense account, your channel will be put into a queue for review. Both automated systems and human reviewers will then review your channel's content before being accepted into the YouTube Partner Program. Note that it can take up to a month for your account to be reviewed; it depends on how many other accounts are in line before you and how much staff is currently available to conduct reviews.

MONETIZING YOUR VIDEOS: Your videos must be monetized for them to start earning income. Monetization means you authorize YouTube to place ads in your videos and agree that no copyrighted materials (music and video clips from TV shows, movies, or other licensed sources) appear in your footage.

If a piece of music accidentally makes it through, YouTube will likely still allow the video to play BUT will not allow ads to be placed on it, meaning you will not make any money from that particular video. These music copyright strikes happened to me frequently when I was vlogging my Walt Disney World vacations, as much of the music played inside the parks was copyrighted. Fortunately, while I could not earn AdSense on those videos, YouTube allowed them to remain on their site. While I could have edited the music out, I chose to keep it in so that I could enjoy it when I watched the videos back myself.

Avoiding copyrighted music is a big reason why many vloggers do voice-overs on their footage. Many stores play music that, if picked up by your camera's microphone, will trigger YouTube to de-monetize your video. Do not worry if this happens; it will not negatively affect your other videos or prevent you from uploading again. It just means that the particular video, or parts of it, will not earn you any AdSense.

If you upload a video that triggers YouTube's copyright system, you can always delete it and re-edit the footage to take the music clips out. If only a small part of your video contains copyrighted music, YouTube can narrow it down for you, and you can choose to have them edit it out for you. This process can take a while, but it is often easier than editing your original footage and reuploading it. And once you have been filming for a while, you will learn where and when to avoid vlogging to prevent copyright issues.

An AdSense account does not automatically mean your videos will earn money, as **you need to monetize each of your videos manually**. This is done in the **YouTube Studio** section of your YouTube account.

You can access your *YouTube Studio* on your desktop computer or via the *YouTube Studio* app. Note that the *YouTube Studio* app is separate from the YouTube app. While I have the *YouTube Studio* app downloaded on my phone, I prefer to use the *YouTube Studio* section on my computer as it is easier to access and edit all available features. The following directions are based on using *YouTube Studio* on a computer, not in the app.

Once a video is uploaded to your YouTube channel, simply click on it, choose the **edit icon** (it looks like a pencil), and then click on the **$ Monetization tab** on the left-hand side of the page. You can monetize your videos through the *YouTube Studio* app, but there are more options on the desktop version.

Clicking on the **$ Monetization** tab will bring up the **Video Monetization** page of your chosen video.

Select **On** from the **Monetization drop-down menu**. The **Type of ads section** will now be accessible for you to select. If your video is over eight minutes long, you will be able to select from the following (or choose all of them):

- **Display ads:** This is the default option that indicates that Google will be placing ads on your videos.
- **Overlay ads:** Overlay image or text ads that can appear on the lower 20% portion of a video. These types of ads appear on videos viewed from a computer, not on mobile or other devices.
- **Sponsored cards:** Sponsored cards are very small call-to-action pop-ups that creators can add to their videos that will take them to past videos they reference or a link to another page the creator wants viewers to visit. These are used mainly for sponsored content.
- **Skippable video ads:** Skippable video ads allow viewers to skip ads after they have been running for 5 sections.
- **Non-skippable video ads:** Non-skippable video ads must be watched before a video can be viewed.

Under the **Type of ads** section is the **Location of video ads** section. Here is where you can choose where ads will be placed in your videos, including:

- **Before video** (pre-roll)
- **During video** (mid-roll)
- **After video** (post-roll)

If your video is over eight minutes long, you will also want to click on the **MANAGE MID-ROLL** option found under **During video (mid-roll).** The advertisements that run in the middle of videos typically bring in the most revenue, so you will want to ensure they are placed effectively in your videos.

YouTube will automatically place mid-roll ads for you as a default option, but I like to make my own selections to ensure that the ads are not too close together. Sometimes YouTube will put in way too many ads or put all the ads right together, which will turn viewers off. Or sometimes they may not put enough ads in. Google also tends to insert ads into strange places within

25

videos, such as at the very end of the video when viewers have already clicked off and are no longer watching.

Depending on the video's length, I typically place my ads every seven to ten minutes. For instance, I will place ads for a fifteen-minute video at the seven-minute mark. If a video is twenty-five minutes long, I might place ads at nine and nineteen minutes.

Placing ad breaks is easy; you simply **click on the "+" next to AD BREAK** and click to add as many individual placements as you want. Then, under the **PLACE AUTOMATICALLY** column, you enter the time stamp for each. You can easily change these, so do not worry about making a mistake.

You can also manually move each ad break at the bottom of the page. I will walk you through the step-by-step process I personally go through to monetize my videos later in this book.

Once you have your ad breaks where you want them, simply click on the **SAVE** button in the top right corner to confirm your selections.

A pop-up box will appear on your screen titled **Tell us what's in your video**. Here you will need to confirm whether your video contains **Inappropriate language, Adult content, Violence, Shocking content, Harmful or dangerous acts, Drug-related content, Hateful Content, Firearms-related content**, and/or **Sensitive issues.** YouTube strictly controls videos that contain any of those types of content, so unless your videos contain any of them, you will simply check **None of the above** before hitting the **Submit** button.

Click **SAVE** again, and you will be done with monetizing your videos!

Make sure to go back into your old videos, the ones that were not monetized initially, to monetize them, too. The mid-roll ads are especially important, so even though it can be time-consuming to update your older videos with them, it will be worth it in terms of your earnings.

Note that I will be going into more detail about how I upload, edit, and prepare my videos in *Chapter Nine: A Day in the Life* to give you a better idea about managing your own uploads.

The steps to set up and monetize your YouTube channel can seem overwhelming for new creators. Signing up for a Google account, an AdSense account, and a YouTube account, plus then applying for the YouTube Partner Program, all take time. And you need to ensure that the information you provide is accurate; after all, you are asking that Google pay you for ads placed in and on your content. It is almost like applying for a job, plus you also need to make sure your tax information is correct.

Be patient, and make sure to follow all the instructions when you are filling out your applications. While signing up for a Google account and YouTube channel are automatic once you have submitted the forms, being accepted into the *YouTube Partner Program* can take a bit of time depending on how many other people are applying, as Google employees manually verify each account. Sometimes it only takes a week for accounts to be verified; other times, it takes a few months. The wait can be frustrating, but once you are monetized and start earning money from your videos, I promise it will be worth it.

And remember that you only must do these tasks once. After you have all your accounts set up and have monetized your YouTube videos, you will be able to relax and enjoy the monthly deposits of money into your bank account!

YOUTUBE DEMOGRAPHICS

- 53.90% of YouTube users are male
- 46.10% of YouTube users are female
- 12% of the YouTube global audience is comprised of males between the ages of 24 and 34 years old
- 9% of the YouTube global audience is comprised of females between the ages of 24 and 34 years old
- 9% of the YouTube global audience is comprised of males between the ages of 35 and 44 years old

- 7.5% of the YouTube global audience is comprised of females between the ages of 35 and 44 years old
- The majority of YouTube users are between the ages of 15 and 35
- 80% of parents in the United States with children aged 11 and under say their children watch YouTube videos
- The average YouTube visitor checks nearly nine YouTube pages per day
- The largest share of YouTube users is in India
- United States, Indonesia, Brazil, Russia, Japan, Mexico, Germany, Pakistan, and Vietnam follow India as the countries with the most YouTuber users

CHAPTER TWO: FILMING EQUIPMENT & SET-UP

My guess is that you are eager to read this section of the book because you want me to tell you exactly which camera you need to purchase to film your videos, the specific software you will need to edit your videos, and the perfect computer you need to edit your videos on, right? Maybe there is even one link where you can buy everything you need with just one click.

Well, I hate to disappoint you as it just is not that easy, because while it would be nice if there were an all-in-one kit you could purchase directly from YouTube to start your channel, the fact is that there are hundreds of different setups available. Every creator runs their channel differently regarding the equipment they use.

The options for filming, editing, and uploading YouTube videos are endless, from different cameras and lighting equipment to editing software and computer systems. And because new products are continually being released, something new and better is always coming out.

However, while the options can seem overwhelming, I will be going over the basics in this chapter. I will give you ideas that range from using what you already own to investing in professional equipment.

You may find that you already own the tools you need to start your channel and that you do not have to purchase anything. I personally film, edit and upload videos on my iPhone, only switching to my laptop to finish some backend work before the video goes live. I have never owned an expensive camera or invested in editing software, and I have successfully built two channels without either. Heck, I don't even own a proper ring light, which is considered a must-have among YouTube creators!

When beginning any new venture, I believe it is always best to start with what you already have before investing in anything new. This chapter will cover the types of products needed to film, edit, and upload YouTube videos, along with examples of the current top products being used by creators. While I cannot tell you the exact setup to use, you will come away with the knowledge of what is out there and can then decide if you want to purchase any of it or if you can make do with what you already own.

As I said, I do all my filming, editing, and uploading on my iPhone. In fact, I have only ever produced my YouTube videos using an iPhone. While I use apps to edit and upload my videos, I use my laptop to complete the back-end production aspects for my channel. In the chapter *A Day in the Life,* which appears later in this book, I will go over the step-by-step process for using an iPhone to film, edit and upload videos. Many YouTube creators start with an iPhone.

Setting aside the iPhone option, however, here is the necessary equipment you will need to run a YouTube channel:

CAMERA: Either an iPhone or a DSLR camera work best for filming YouTube videos. Many successful YouTube creators offer videos explaining their filming process along with the cameras they use. The best advice I can give you is to search YouTube for "best cameras to film YouTube videos" to see what comes up. Look for the most recent videos to provide information on the latest models. DSLR cameras range from $100 to well over $2,000.

You can purchase brand-new cameras, of course, or you can search on Ebay for secondhand models for much less. You will find tutorial videos on YouTube of nearly every camera ever made, so you will be able to find help regardless of what camera you eventually end up with.

As a basic guideline, you want a camera that can film in HD, whether 720p or 1080p. HD (high definition) is the highest quality filming available for personal cameras and results in video footage that appears super crisp and clear.

Most phones even film in HD these days, including the iPhone I use. While I upload from my iPhone directly to YouTube, you will need to transfer your video footage to your computer via the camera's SD memory card if you use a stand-alone camera. Most creators who use this method rely on memory cards to hold and transfer footage and multiple batteries to keep their cameras working. And some creators still film additional footage on their phones.

The most popular DSLR cameras currently being used to make YouTube videos are:

1. **Canon PowerShot G7 X Mark III:** A compact favorite of vloggers who film in 4K with a starting price of $600.
2. **Sony ZV-1:** Another compact video camera with 4K video resolution and a starting price of $700.
3. **DJI Pocket 2:** Offers excellent stabilization and straightforward operation with a starting price of $350.
4. **GoPro Hero2:** Popular because of its excellent stabilization, but you may want to add an external microphone. The price starts at $400.

5. **DJI Osmo Action:** Dubbed the "best YouTube action camera for novices," this waterproof camera is super affordable at under $200.
6. **Sony A6600:** One of the most expensive vlogging cameras available at under $1400. However, the battery life and storage make it popular for taking a lot of footage.
7. **Canon EOS M6 Mark II:** High-resolution camera starting at $800.
8. **Panasonic Lumix GH5 II:** A great choice for both still shots and video, but with a hefty starting price of $2000.
9. **Sigma fp:** The smallest full-frame camera also streams over USB and has a starting price of $1700.
10. **Samsung Galaxy S21 Ultra:** This phone also shoots in 8K, making it even better than the iPhone, with a price of $900.

If you already own a DSLR camera, see if you can use it for filming before investing in a new model. Again, do a YouTube search of the model camera you own and see if you can find tutorials about how to use it for filming videos. Chances are, at least one other person is filming their YouTube videos with the same camera you already own.

LIGHTING EQUIPMENT: If you intend to film vlog-style videos, i.e., footage of you as you go about your everyday life, then you will not have to worry about purchasing lighting equipment as you will be using whatever light happens to be available in the setting you are filming in, including natural light. There are small ring lights that you can attach to your camera or phone to provide better lighting if you need it.

If you plan to film exclusively inside, you can purchase several kinds of lights, everything from single-ring lights to multi-lighting systems. However, if you have a large window that lets in a lot of natural light, you may be able to get away using just the window for lighting when filming sit-down videos inside.

Note that even if you have a window with natural light, you may still want some additional lighting when filming. Many YouTube creators use studio lighting or a "ring light" when they film. Ring lights vary in size from tabletop to floor length. You can even purchase small ring lights that attach to your iPhone.

A search of "YouTube lights" on Amazon or other tech shopping sites will bring up a long list of options with prices from $30 and going up into the hundreds. Options range from single-light setups to complex multi-piece systems. A simple 10" ring light with a tripod stand is a great option to start with. As I suggested with cameras, search YouTube for "video lighting" to see suggestions from other creators.

Small ring lights are becoming more and more commonplace, meaning you can find portable ones for as low as $5 at Target, Walmart, and even dollar stores. However, remember that you get what you pay for. A ring light that doesn't properly attach to your camera or stand well is a waste of money, especially when you could have purchased a better-quality light for not a lot more money.

Remember again that it is okay to start with what you have. A window and a lamp can do wonders for your video lighting. I film my indoor at-home videos using natural light supplemented by lamps. And I don't use extra lighting when filming outside of my home, whether I am indoors or out. As your YouTube journey progresses, you can always explore more expensive options if you feel they are necessary.

MICROPHONE: When it comes to filming YouTube videos, iPhones and most digital cameras come with built-in microphones. However, as you continue your YouTube journey, you may want to invest in additional microphones, both for sit-down videos and when you are vlogging.

Microphones come in all configurations, from desktop models, headsets, portable, noise buffering, and even clip-on. Prices vary wildly, too.

If a separate microphone will benefit you is something you will likely only discover after you have been creating videos for a while. For instance, if you film mostly vlog-style videos, you may want a microphone with a windscreen (a busy little attachment that looks like a rabbit foot) as it will help filter out background noise such as wind.

If you find yourself drawn to creating sit-down videos and even interviews, a desktop microphone might become something you feel you need for your business.

Microphones, like ring lights and fancy cameras, are things you can add later in your YouTube career. Unless your phone or camera cannot record sound, there is no need to invest in one right away.

VIDEO EDITING SOFTWARE: These days, there are a lot of options when it comes to video editing software. I personally just use the free **iMovie app** on my iPhone to edit my YouTube videos. The iMovie app is also available for Apple laptops and computers. It is the most popular video editing software as it is easy to use and comes with most Mac computer systems.

If you cannot or do not want to use iMovie, there are other options available, including:

- **Premiere Pro:** Available for both Windows and Mac, Premiere Pro is a favorite among YouTube creators. Subscriptions start at $21 a month and go up depending on features.
- **Final Cut Pro:** Available for Mac only for a one-time cost of $299.99 directly from Apple. Final Cut Pro is used by professional film editors and YouTuber creators but might be too sophisticated for newbies.
- **Premiere Elements**: Available for both Windows and Mac for a one-time cost of $99.99 from Adobe. The

simple interface is suitable for beginners as it is a watered-down version of Premiere Pro.
- **Pinnacle Studio 24**: Available for Windows. Prices start at $45, depending on the store. Pinnacle Studio is an excellent option for beginners.
- **CyberLink Power Director 365**: Available for both Windows and Mac starting at $29.99 a month. It is easy to use but also offers some advanced options.
- **Premiere Rush**: Available for Android and iOS from $9.99 to $52.99 per month. If you want to use your Android device to film videos, this is the app you want to use.
- **Vimeo**: This lets you piece photos and videos together and adds other elements. They offer a free version and paid plans of $55 a month.

I suggest you do the same for video editing software as I recommended for vlogging cameras and lighting: Do your research by seeing what other YouTube creators are using. A simple search of "best video editing software" on YouTube will yield many results. Many YouTube creators also put links to the items they use in the description boxes under their videos.

See if some channels you currently enjoy watching have their editing software linked. You may find that you already have an editing program installed, one that came with your computer. Again, do a YouTube search of what you already have to see if other YouTube creators are also using the same program.

As with cameras, new software options and updates are continually being released. Plus, what software you need depends on your computer system (Mac or PC) and your skill level. As always, see if you have something already installed on your phone or computer that will work before investing in new software.

COMPUTER: While I do most of my YouTube work on my iPhone, I still utilize my laptop for my videos. I find it much easier to type in my titles and description box information using my computer versus my small phone keyboard. I also like accessing the *YouTube Studio* feature from my desktop to adjust my video specifics and monetization settings. While there is a *YouTube Studio* app on my iPhone, I still prefer the full version of the full website for completing specific tasks.

Fortunately, *YouTube Studio* is accessible via the internet and works with Macs and PCs. So, the computer you use for editing videos will work just fine for any other YouTube work you do as long as it has an internet connection.

While I use my Apple iPhone to film, edit, and upload my videos, I use a Dell laptop with Microsoft software to access the internet and complete the backend work on my videos. Yes, I use a combination of both Apple and Microsoft products to manage my YouTube channel!

While most large YouTube channels rely on Mac computers to edit, there are options for PC users as well. The Microsoft Surface, HP, and Dell computers (which I am a personal fan of) are used by many creators. A powerful and fast processor is the most critical factor you will want to consider in any computer you intend to use to run a YouTube channel (or, frankly, any online business). When I purchase a new computer, I buy one with the fastest processor I can afford as process speed affects all of my computer work, not just YouTube.

If you are completely clueless about computers, simply visit a store that sells computers, such as Apple or Best Buy, and ask an associate which models have the most powerful and fastest processors. Tell them you will be using the computer to edit and upload videos. Office supply stores such as Staples and OfficeMax also have a large selection of computers and associates who can assist you.

A few years back, I needed to upgrade my laptop, and I asked an associate at Sam's Club which laptop had the best processor. He showed me their two best options, and I chose from there. Now

I typically only buy my computers from Sam's Club as they have the best prices. Costco also has great deals on computers.

If you already use your computer for gaming, it is likely powerful enough to handle YouTube, too. And the speed and power of your computer are really only important if you plan to edit and upload videos on it.

INTERNET CONNECTION: Having a fast, reliable internet connection is essential if you intend to use your computer to edit and upload videos. I use my iPhone because the upload speed is considerably higher than if I uploaded videos on my laptop. If you are an avid YouTube watcher, you have likely heard creators complain about the time it takes to upload their videos. So, if you still use a dial-up modem to access the World Wide Web, it is time to upgrade.

These days, most internet service providers offer various speeds of high-speed internet. I recommend going with the fastest one you can afford. I firmly believe that time is money, and I need my internet connection to work as quickly as possible for me to run all my businesses, including YouTube.

If you do not have internet access where you live and cannot obtain it, you can access the internet at your local library. Many public places now also have free WIFI. And if you are using your iPhone to film, edit, and upload videos, you only need your cell service to complete most YouTube tasks. I have high-speed internet at home, but if it goes out, I use the hot spot feature on my iPhone to get internet access back on my computer.

TRIPOD: Tripods are another item you might be able to delay buying or skip altogether. If you plan only to vlog, your hand will serve as your tripod. However, I do have a hand-help grip that I use on my phone when vlogging. It also works as a stand as it holds my phone upright when I am filming a sit-down video.

I went for years without a tripod but finally spent $70 on a good model with a solid base and a ring light attached. However, for years I just propped my phone up on books and boxes in order to film!

I have seen YouTube creators prop their cameras and phones up in various ways: on stacks of books, nestled into cabinets, even on open shelves. If you buy a lighting kit, even a basic ring light, it will often come with a tripod to which you can attach a camera or phone. There are even portable tripods that come with a small ring light attached for use when you are on the go.

The benefits of a tripod are that they keep your filming device steady and set at the angle you choose. It can be a little more work to get the right angle when you simply set your camera onto a flat surface or what you think is a flat surface. I still run into issues keeping my camera steady on a table even when using my new stand, as the table itself is unsteady. Even with a new device, I sometimes still just prop my phone up to film.

See how you get by without using a tripod before buying one. There are all styles and sizes available on sites like Amazon that start at around $15. However, I recommend investing in something with a weighted bottom to keep the camera steady.

TO RECAP: Figuring out which camera you will be filming on, what editing software you need, and if there are accessories such as lights and tripods that will help you create videos can feel like overwhelming and expensive choices to make. Start with what you have and invest in better equipment as your YouTube journey continues!

WHAT YOUTUBE VIEWERS ARE WATCHING:

- *Despacito* on Luis Fonsi's channel is the most liked YouTube video and has nearly 8 billion views
- YouTube Rewind 2018 is the most disliked YouTube video
- The number one YouTube channel based on subscribers is T-Series, with 213 million
- YouTube Movies is the second most popular channel,

- with 150 million subscribers
- Cocomelon is the third most popular channel with 133 million subscribers
- Baby Shark Dance is the most viewed YouTube video with nearly 11 billion views
- Commentary, music videos, reviews, tutorials, and comedy are the top five most popular YouTube categories

CHAPTER THREE: FILMING TIPS

So, you have figured out which camera, lighting, editing software, computer, and tripod you will use for your YouTube channel. That covers the equipment side of things. But there are other things to consider when you are filming YouTube videos that do not cost you any money but are just as important as those. And these are things that you will only learn through trial and error. Your first few attempts at filming likely won't be your best, but they will be a valuable learning experience for you.

Quality: No matter what equipment you use to film, edit, and upload your YouTube videos, producing high-quality videos is vital. As I have said several times, you do not need to invest in fancy equipment, at least not initially, so you must do the very best you can with what you have. You don't need the most expensive camera to make quality videos.

Even though I film on my iPhone, I still upload my videos in High Definition. iPhones let you film in 720p, 1080p, and 4K. Choose 4K if possible, although both 720p and 1080p are still excellent. The difference will come in the upload speed. I often do not have the time to allow my videos to upload in 1080p or 4K as I need my iPhone for other work.

But if you have the option, always choose the highest resolution possible. YouTube and viewers both favor videos shot in the highest definition possible. If I have a particularly long video, I will turn the screensaver off, plug my phone into a charger, and start the upload process to run overnight.

A Steady Hand: Nothing is worse than watching shaky camera footage, and I have been guilty of doing this myself while vlogging. A hand-held stand or tripod can help tremendously with this, which is why I now have a small handheld stand that is attached to my phone.

If you are filming a sit-down video with the camera in one place, make sure it is on a flat, steady surface and that it is not moving around while you are filming. Placing your computer at eye level is important, even if that means you prop your iPhone up on a stack of books.

I also run into issues of accidentally getting my fingers in the shot while filming with my iPhone. Sometimes I realize I want to vlog something but forgot my hand-help tripod. I end up placing my finger too close to the lens, and images of my blurry finger appear in the picture. I can't tell you how many times I've had to delete otherwise good footage because of my own blurry finger!

Light: Lighting is the biggest issue for most YouTube creators, me included. As I discussed earlier, natural light (either outside or through a window) can provide you with excellent lighting, although you may decide to upgrade to professional lights. Ring lights come in all sizes, from small portable versions attached to your iPhone to full-size models that take up half a room.

I rely on natural light when vlogging outdoors, and stores are often well-lit enough for me if I am vlogging while shopping. At home, I rely on a large window and a lamp. Whether you decide to invest in lighting or make do with what you have on hand, making sure your videos are well-lit is essential to your channel growth. Having light in front of you, rather than behind, will illuminate your face versus creating a shadow.

Most cameras and phones come with flash settings that can help illuminate your setting and cause things to look unnatural. Eyes, for one thing, can appear red when a flash is used.

Speak Up: A big problem I see with many new YouTube creators is their low video volume; I cannot even hear what they are saying. When filming, make sure you speak in a clear, loud voice. While you do not want to scream at your viewers, you want to make sure they can hear what you are saying.

Talking too fast or too slow can also turn off viewers. I struggle with speaking too quickly and must continually remind myself to slow my speech and speak reasonably, making sure to enunciate my words so that viewers can understand what I am saying.

Ensure there is no background noise while filming, such as music or the television. Not only will background noise interfere with viewers hearing what you are saying, but often background noise is copyrighted, which means it may prevent you from monetizing your videos. If you are filming in public, there will likely be background noise. Make sure you hold your camera close when speaking to ensure your viewers hear you over the noise.

You can also do voiceovers for videos filmed in very loud locations. If you are filming in a store where the music is very loud, you can film your footage but then do a voiceover during the editing process.

If filming at home, turn your phone to silent and film in a quiet room with a closed door. If you live with other people, let them know when you are filming and ask them to keep noise and interruptions to a minimum. If you have a dog that barks or pets that will distract you, it may be best to place them elsewhere in your home while filming.

I have dogs, so trust me when I say they can be as distracting as young children when I try to film. I schedule my at-home filming during times when they are napping. Stay-at-home parents may reserve their filming for when their children are in school. Removing distractions also means your filming process will go much faster, so you can get back to your family and pets sooner.

If you are vlogging, ensure your hand does not inadvertently cover up the microphone. Also, please be aware that most music is copyrighted, meaning you will not be able to monetize videos where background music is being played, such as in stores or tourist attractions. As I mentioned, you may need to do voiceover commentary or overlay the footage with music that has a free license.

The most challenging part of vlogging is ensuring the microphone picks up no copyrighted music. Nothing is worse than taking the time to vlog only to have YouTube put a copyright strike on the video due to music in the background. While the video will usually still be eligible to be viewed, it will be ineligible to earn you any AdSense.

I've had entire Disney vlogs demonetized due to the music. One trick you can use is to have YouTube narrow down where copyrighted music is in your video and allow them to trim it out. This process can take a day or two, but it can save a video you've already finished versus refilming it.

Making sure you speak clearly is also essential when filming videos. As I mentioned, in my everyday life, I tend to talk fast and fill my speech with slang. But to appeal to a worldwide audience, I make sure to speak slowly and clearly and avoid saying "like" and "um" throughout my videos.

I also edit out sneezes and coughs. Having some water nearby is helpful to stay hydrated while filming so that your speech remains as clear as possible. Lip balm is also handy to keep your lips from drying out, which can negatively affect your speech.

Backgrounds: You have likely seen YouTube videos with professionally designed backgrounds and those shot in what looks like a hoarder's home. While you do not need to spend thousands of dollars to make the background of your videos look like it came straight from a home decor magazine, you want to make sure to film in a clean, clutter-free space with a simple backdrop.

I have a dedicated space in my office where I film sit-down videos. I have bookshelves behind me, and I change the décor on the shelves seasonally. In the past, I will admit that my backgrounds were not as nice as I would have liked them to be, especially ones where there were piles of Ebay inventory behind me (although, in my defense, I was filming videos about Ebay!).

You want your background to complement the subject of your videos. My Ebay videos were a bit cluttered, but, again, Ebay was my full-time job, and other Ebay sellers watched my videos. So, it wasn't as big of an issue. But if you are filming cooking videos, you don't want viewers to see a dirty kitchen. If you are filming a tutorial about a specific product, you don't want a bunch of non-related items clogging up the screen.

I am always trying to improve the quality of my videos, including my backgrounds. Note that if you are vlogging, you do not have to worry about creating a pretty backdrop as you will be filming yourself in whatever place you happen to be. However, you still want to be aware of your surroundings so that viewers focus on you, not on what might be happening in the shot behind you.

Try not to film other people in your vlogs, such as other customers, inside of a store. While it is normal to catch a glimpse of a stranger's back in a vlog, you do not want a video filmed with a stranger's face looking right into the camera. Many people vlog with the camera lens focused on them, while others may film with someone else, and the person with the camera focuses on the second person.

One of my favorite backgrounds that I see many female YouTubers use is to film with their bed behind them, and twinkle lights (the kind you put on Christmas trees) strung up around the bed frame or window. This lighting arrangement creates such a lovely scene for filming. Shelves with minimal decorations also create a nice backdrop.

Other people film with the nicest part of their kitchen or living room behind them. Gamers and review channels often have bookshelves behind them full of neatly arranged products. Beauty channels often have some makeup products in the background. You want your background to align with your content. For instance, if you film cooking videos, you will want to use your kitchen as your backdrop, not your dirty garage.

When in doubt, a plain wall always makes a great backdrop, especially if it is next to a window that provides natural light. If you are filming in a room with sparse decorations and furniture, test your audio to make sure there is no echo when speaking. Adding a rug on top of a hardwood floor can help buffer an echo in an empty room.

Suppose you are serious about making YouTube a business that earns you a decent income. In that case, you will want to consider dedicating a space for filming that is well-lit and nicely decorated. However, if you are just starting out or are only interested in making a bit of money from YouTube, do your best with what you have.

Some of the biggest YouTube channels on the site today got their start with the creators filming while sitting on the floor of their bedrooms or even sitting in their cars with the cameras propped up on their steering wheels. I've seen full-time YouTube creators film their videos with their cameras stacked atop empty shoe boxes. As I have already mentioned several times, start with what you have and build from there.

Camera Angle: Finding the angle from which you look your best on camera can be challenging. Most of us feel we have a "good side," the side of our face from which we look a bit more attractive than the other. However, video is much different from

45

still photography in that you move around on film and are not sitting in a stationary position. Therefore, it is more important to have the camera facing you directly and slightly above you. Having to look up a bit to the camera helps eliminate the double chin phenomenon!

As with the background, the camera angle is something I have constantly been challenged by. I've tried numerous tripods over the years for my iPhone, but most were flimsy. I finally invested in a $70 model with a strong base that holds my phone steady and has an attached ring light. However, I still sometimes find myself propping my phone up on a stack of books to film.

When vlogging, I now have a portable hand-held tripod that I can attach to my phone that also converts to a stand; I can just prop the stand up on a flat surface to film when I am on the go. And the handle helps me hold the camera steady when I am vlogging.

Of course, if you choose not to appear on screen, you need not focus on how you look but on what you are filming, whether a single stationary item or a moving scene. For instance, if you are filming cooking videos, you will want a tripod holding the camera to look over what you are preparing. Or perhaps you can have someone else hold the camera and film you.

If you are doing close-up shots of your hands, make sure your nails are trim and clean. Nothing turns viewers off more than dirty fingernails. If you are filming your hands a lot, a professional manicure is a good investment, and it is also a tax write-off as it is a business expense! Also, make sure your clothes are clean and tidy.

Do not be surprised if your first videos do not look that great, as it takes time to learn how to film best. Try different angles and methods until you find what you are most comfortable with. I have put many of my older videos on "private," as the quality is terrible!

Keep It Classy: While you do not have to have your hair and make-up professionally done every time you film a YouTube video, you do want to take care of your appearance. Looking as clean and neat as possible goes a long way toward presenting yourself in the best possible light, even if you are simply wearing jeans and a plain tee shirt.

If you smoke, do not smoke on camera. Avoid chewing gum while filming. Be aware of your language; swearing not only turns off viewers but it can result in YouTube demonetizing your videos. And do your best to clean up your surrounding area. No one wants to see your overflowing trash can or a pile of dirty laundry in the background of your videos.

As I mentioned earlier, clean nails are so important, especially if you are filming close-up shots with your hands. Try to prepare yourself as you would if you were going on a job interview or first date when your clothing and appearance are at your best. You don't have to have a full face of makeup or have your hair professionally styled, but a clean face and freshly brushed hair are a must. Remember that you are trying to appeal to a broad audience of viewers and present yourself accordingly.

Preview Before Uploading: I have watched some horrible YouTube videos over the years, ones where the footage is dark, the volume is on mute, and the screen is jerky. I have even seen videos that were upside down! Before you make your videos live, preview them first. While they do not have to be up to the Hollywood standard of film quality, you want them to be as clear and steady as possible. If a video looks terrible to you while previewing it, imagine what viewers will think when you upload it.

Redo videos that are not of good quality. Practice makes perfect! I have re-filmed many videos during my time on YouTube. I know that having to re-film a video is frustrating. Still, I would rather take the time to completely redo a video than have a poor-quality clip be viewed by thousands and potentially millions of people. One poorly filmed video could cost me, new subscribers. Therefore, I would rather have no video than a poorly filmed one.

YOUTUBE CREATOR AWARDS:

- The **Silver Creator Award is** given to channels when they reach 100K subscribers
- The **Gold Creator Award** is given to channels when they reach 1 million subscribers
- The **Diamond Creator Award** is given to channels when they reach 10 million subscribers

CHAPTER FOUR: YOUR CHANNEL'S THEME & CONTENT

As I talked about in the Introduction of this book, my first YouTube channel was dedicated solely to my reselling business on Ebay. My videos showed viewers the items I sourced at estate sales and thrift stores to sell online, along with all my tips and tricks for making money on Ebay. I did not really talk about anything else but reselling on that channel, and the people who subscribed to me were there to learn and/or talk about just Ebay, too.

I had also talked about how when I started my first YouTube channel that I signed up under a non-Google email (which, I remind you, you can no longer do; so, no worries that you will make the same mistake that I did) and that I was not able to monetize my first channel. It took starting a second channel under a Google account that allowed me to earn AdSense income from my videos.

But to be honest, when I first started YouTube, I was unaware that you could make money on the site. I was happy to just connect with other resellers and share what I knew. It was a small community, and it really helped me change the direction of my online selling business. If you will remember from the *Introduction*, I was struggling to figure out a new direction for my business; the videos I found on YouTube helped me do just that.

However, I will also be honest and tell you that once I realized the possibility of making money on YouTube, I made the leap and started a new channel. I deleted the first channel and focused on my newly created one because I still enjoyed being on the site and wanted to earn money from my videos. However, just as I had with the first channel, my content still mainly centered around Ebay.

That changed over the years, as I have already discussed. From reselling content to couponing and traveling to cooking, my content across my current two active channels has been all over the place. And that has caused my channels to struggle. The constant change in content and my posting schedule threw my YouTube algorithm for a loop, and YouTube punished me by suppressing my channels and placing low-dollar ads on my videos.

However, you do not have to make the same mistakes I have. I have learned the hard way what works and what does not, and this book is my way of passing that information on to you. Not that you won't make mistakes along the way. We all do. But I hope you can look at those mistakes as learning lessons. Fortunately, if you are just starting your YouTube journey, millions of other creators have paved the way for you, whose lessons you can learn from.

So, what is the biggest lesson I can share with you?

Figure out your channel's theme and stick to it!

Mixing business content with lifestyle content did not work for me, and my AdSense earnings dropped because of it. You need to figure out exactly what your channel is about in order to grow your audience and income. And if you want to create drastically different content than you started with, you can do that on a second or even third channel.

Now, that does not mean you cannot film different types of videos on one channel. It just means you need to stick to one TOPIC for your channel. For instance, I have many friends who are resellers who produce lots of different types of videos, such as "shop with me" vlogs where they go sourcing, sit-down haul videos where they share what they purchased to resell, and even live sales where viewers buy directly from them in real-time.

But while the *styles* of videos may differ, the *topic* is always the same: reselling. Those who share lifestyle videos do so on a second channel. You have likely also seen this from some of the YouTube creators you follow. Many, like me, have a channel for vlogs and a channel for sit-down videos. Some focus on one topic on one channel, such as gaming or makeup tutorials, and something absolutely different on another channel, such as travel vlogs or parenting advice. You can cover different topics on YouTube as long as you cover each on different channels.

For me, I did best when I kept my reselling content to one channel and my lifestyle content to another. While some viewers watch all of my videos regardless of topic or channel, some only tune in for the reselling videos and others are only interested in non-reselling videos. Two different audiences plus two different topics equal TWO different YouTube channels.

To choose your video's category, log into your YouTube account, click on your profile icon, and then click on **YouTube Studio**. Click on **Content** to bring up your list of videos.

If you want each of your videos to be placed in different categories, you'll need to do each one individually. Click on the box on the left side next to the video and then click on **Edit** at the top of the page. Select **Category** from the drop-down menu. A new drop-down menu will appear with the **15 YouTube categories**, which we discuss further in the following section.

If you want to put all of your videos in the same category, simply select all of your videos and then click on **Edit** at the top of the page. Select **Category** from the drop-down menu and select the category to which you want your videos added.

Whether you edit each video individually or do a bulk edit, you will click on **UPDATE VIDEOS** to finish to process.

The 15 YouTube Categories: You can choose a category for your channel and individual videos. The categories are in no particular order.

1. **Film & Animation:** Movie trailers, full movies, movies scenes, songs, behind-the-scenes videos, and anything related to films
2. **Autos & Vehicles:** Vehicle reviews, advertising, and vlogging
3. **Music:** Music videos and concert vlogs
4. **Pets & Animals:** Pet and animal education as well as pet vlogging
5. **Sports:** Athlete interviews, sporting events, and collecting
6. **Travel & Events:** Vacation vlogs, festivals, and travel advice
7. **Gaming:** Video games
8. **People & Blogs:** Everything from parenting and beauty to health and fitness
9. **Comedy:** Spoofs and pranks
10. **Entertainment:** Television, celebrities, and gossip
11. **News & Politics:** Current events
12. **How-to & Style:** Tutorials, fashion, organization, and home
13. **Education:** Home-schooling, teaching, lectures, and history
14. **Science & Technology:** Space, new inventions, and educational content

15. **Nonprofits & Activism:** Social causes

Starting out, I would recommend you begin with just ONE YouTube channel and commit to focusing on one category. You want to master running a single channel and learning one category before thinking about having two...or more. Yes, some people have three or even four channels. However, most YouTube creators only have one channel, so do not panic if you can only see yourself with one, as it is totally normal.

You may start your channel creating one type of content but quickly realize it's not for you. It's okay to change course in the beginning before you have built up an audience. You just don't want to change from filming prank videos to creating gardening videos after you've built up your channel on the former over several years.

If I were only making videos about Ebay, I would only have one channel. Reselling is such a small niche that it really does well with a dedicated channel, meaning it is best for me to put other content on a separate channel. I started my second channel because I wanted to create non-reselling content.

But if the videos you intend to share all fall under the same general theme, such as lifestyle or gaming, then you will be just fine with all your content on one channel. And it's not like you can't mix some other content within the same video. Maybe you normally film makeup tutorials but take a yearly vacation to Walt Disney World. You could easily add a vacation vlog into your schedule without completely throwing off your algorithm. And you never know: sometimes, what you think your viewers won't be interested in ends up being more popular than what you've been uploading!

When I first started on YouTube, I viewed having a channel like having your own television network. I thought that my channel was like a network in my cable lineup. I believed that I could have different types of "shows" on my channel and that viewers would just pick the videos they wanted to watch.

Unfortunately, that is not the way viewers behave on YouTube. While you have ABC in your television channel line-up, it is likely that you only watch a few of the shows on the ABC network. However, you do not take ABC out of your television package just because you do not watch every show they air. You watch the shows you want to and simply ignore the rest.

YouTube, however, is different. Viewers look at the entire YouTube site as if it were a television network, with the individual channels functioning as separate shows. They view YouTube like ABC; they have the YouTube app installed on their phone the way we have ABC automatically in our television line-up. And just like ABC has different types of television shows, YouTube has different types of channels.

You have YouTube on your smartphone or computer and watch the "shows," i.e., the channels you like. However, you do not watch ALL the channels because you are not interested in all the different "shows." But you keep YouTube installed on your devices the same way you keep the various networks, such as ABC, installed on your television lineup.

Think of it like this: Say your favorite television show is *Grey's Anatomy*. *Grey's Anatomy* still airs on the ABC television network, but it is now also shown on many other channels and even streaming services via syndication. Imagine if you were happily watching an episode of *Grey's Anatomy*, but then the following show to air was *Dancing with the Stars*, another ABC staple. Now, you may like *Dancing with the Star*, but for this example, let's say that you do not. If you were watching *Grey's Anatomy* on your television or streaming service and *Dancing with the Stars* suddenly came on, you would just change the channel to a different show, right?

However, what if *Grey's Anatomy* had its very own dedicated television channel? You need to subscribe to this channel separately from your other television channels. But since *Grey's Anatomy* is your absolute favorite show, you are thrilled to be able to subscribe to a channel that is dedicated only to *Grey's Anatomy*.

But imagine one day that when you went to watch *Grey's Anatomy* on this dedicated channel, they suddenly started showing Dancing with the Stars episode*s*.

Suddenly this unique channel that you only subscribed to so that you could watch Grey's Anatomy is showing you a completely different show, making it hard for you even to find the episodes of *Grey's Anatomy* that you want to watch.

Would you stay subscribed to the channel or look for better content elsewhere? If this select *Grey's Anatomy* channel were a YouTube channel, most YouTube subscribers would unsubscribe once other shows were introduced. They would then find a different channel focused only on *Grey's Anatomy*, leaving the first channel to die out.

Some YouTube viewers will subscribe and stay subscribed to channels because they like all or at least most of the "shows" (individual videos) that are being uploaded. However, suppose they start to dislike more "shows" (individual videos) than they actually like. In that case, they may unsubscribe from that channel and search out different channels to subscribe to, ones that provide them with the content they want.

You want to keep your audience and not drive them away, which is why it is so important to stick to the theme of your channel! If you have a beauty channel, stick to beauty-related content. If you have a travel channel, stick to travel-related content.

The most loyal of my YouTube viewers watch most videos I put out across both of my channels. Some viewers watch all the videos on both of my channels, while others only watch one channel. And still, others only check in periodically depending on the video *topic*. But most of my subscribers choose one channel or the other – not both.

Trying to mix vacation vlogs with reselling videos was a

disaster for me as it confused my viewers as to what my channel (i.e., the "shows") was about, and I lost subscribers on both channels because of it. And when I tried to rebrand my channels completely (I dabbled in everything from product reviews, subscription boxes, shopping hauls, and even a reselling Podcast), I further lost viewers. And when subscribers dropped off, YouTube stopped showing my videos to potential new viewers.

I had to regroup and start fresh, committing to ONE type of content for each channel and sticking to those categories, even if that meant I was starting from scratch to rebuild my viewership. Just because my main channel has nearly 28,000 subscribers doesn't mean my videos get 28,000 views. When I was changing my content, I was lucky to get 1,000 views on a video. It was a scary time, and it almost made me quit YouTube.

These days I have my main channel, *Ann Eckhart*, where I film sit-down videos, and I have a second channel, *Ann Eckhart Vlogs*, for vlogging videos. Some viewers love vlogs; some viewers hate them. Some viewers love sit-down videos; other viewers hate them. Having two separate channels ensures that I keep both audiences happy and helps me attract new viewers who are looking for specific content (i.e., "shows"). And the YouTube Studio, both on desktop and via the app, makes switching back and forth between my channels quick and easy.

However, at the end of the day, no matter what topic I am filming a video about or how much engagement I am getting between my channels, I try only to make videos that I WANT to make, ones that are FUN and INTERESTING to me. Even though I am now earning money on YouTube, I mainly make videos for my own personal enjoyment.

YouTube has improved my public speaking skills and increased my confidence. It has allowed me to network and make new friends with people I would have never met otherwise. And it has also helped me grow my book sales, make money from sponsorships, get free products, and in 2022, launch an Etsy shop. I make YouTube videos for FUN, and as a bonus, I also earn a PROFIT, and they are a form of advertising for all of my businesses.

While I have covered a wide variety of topics in my years on YouTube, you are likely looking to only film videos on one subject. Do not follow the trends to go with what is popular. Make videos about what you LOVE, and the subscribers, and AdSense revenue, will follow.

Beauty, pranks, and gaming are huge categories on YouTube. But if you have no interest in them, why would you want to make videos on those topics? You may think that whatever it is you are interested in won't have an audience, but you yourself are interested in it means there are other like-minded people just waiting for your content.

Every YouTube category has numerous themes that fall under it. Figuring out your channel's category is relatively easy; it's choosing the theme of your actual videos that can be tricky. Think about how viewers would describe your videos. Most viewers will think about your content in terms of theme, not necessarily categories.

Some common YouTube channel themes and video topics are as follows.

Beauty: Beauty bloggers and vloggers are all over YouTube, and they are some of the most successful channels on the site. Some YouTube "beauty gurus" have an accompanying blog to support their videos and to also earn more ad revenue from their websites, but that seems to be a less popular option than it once was. Instead, YouTube creators are now using Instagram and TikTok to promote their channels.

Regardless, if you love make-up and skincare, sharing your personal tips and tricks with others may be the perfect theme for your channel. And the opportunities for content are endless, as is the possibility of brands sending you free makeup products to test on camera. Beauty channels receive the largest number of free product offers as makeup brands love the chance to have their products featured on YouTube.

In addition to doing make-up tutorials, beauty gurus also do first impression reviews of products, shopping hauls (from stores such as ULTA, Sephora, and Bath & Body Works), make-up storage, and make-up collections. Nail art also falls under the beauty umbrella, and there are entire channels devoted to nail polish storage and application.

The beauty category is very crowded on YouTube. Only start a beauty channel because you LOVE cosmetics, as the chances of success are much lower versus other themes. However, if you are good at applying makeup and have a style that impresses others, the subscribers and ad revenue will follow.

10 Popular Beauty Channels:

1. Sandra Cires Art
2. Jeffree Star
3. Musas
4. Nikkie Tutorials
5. Narins Beauty
6. HellomaphieMX
7. Franciny Ehlke
8. Mari Maria
9. Shruti Arjun Anand
10. Niki and Gabi

Business: A lot of my YouTube videos over the years have fallen under the "Business" category. In addition to reselling, I am also an author and have shared videos about how I make money self-publishing. Other business topics I have made videos about include affiliate marketing, print-on-demand, blogging, and now how to run an Etsy sticker shop.

If you are in a career that others are interested in, consider sharing about it on YouTube. You may even find yourself developing courses and paid Patreon groups based on your knowledge that you can also monetize.

For instance, some of my fellow resellers have private groups that share where to source clothing from and which brands to buy. Viewers must pay for this special access, giving the channel creators an additional income stream. Other friends have created courses and have Patreon groups and merchandise, all of which earn them extra income.

10 Popular Business Channels:

1. Business Insider
2. Gary Vaynerchuk
3. Entrepreneur
4. Brian Tracy
5. Marie Forleo
6. Stanford Business
7. Grant Cardone
8. The Dave Ramsey Show
9. Young Entrepreneurs Forum
10. Google Business

Comedy & Pranks: Pranking has become a hot trend on YouTube, and some creators are making big money by putting on elaborate, often dangerous, and expensive stunts. And while this type of content is not easy to replicate, it can be done on a small scale through sketch comedy or single joke-telling. Videos like these have been an avenue for comedians looking to break into the comedy business.

Note that punk videos are geared toward children and families, and other punk videos are geared toward adults. Your channel should only focus on one of these demographics.

10 Popular Comedy/Prank Channels

1. Roman Atwood
2. VitalyzdTV

3. Just for Laughs Gags
4. Prank ON!
5. Coby Persin
6. LAHWF
7. Jack Vale Films
8. The Flash Family
9. Whatever
10. Chris Chann

Cooking & Baking: Do you love to cook up new recipes or share your favorite baking creations with friends? If you enjoy being in the kitchen, you can share your culinary knowledge via YouTube videos. You do not have to be an expert chef, either; even the most straightforward recipes are popular on YouTube. In fact, sometimes simple is best as people are looking for quick and easy meal ideas.

I have posted several cooking and baking videos on my channels over the years; all my recipes are super easy to make, and I always get a lot of great feedback from viewers. Most of these videos are relatively short in length, but they are some of my top-earning AdSense videos!

If you start a cooking channel, you'll also want to create an Amazon Affiliate account so that you can link the kitchen tools you use in your videos. These links can generate you additional income when people click through to Amazon and make a purchase.

10 Popular Cooking/Baking Channels:

1. Binging with Babish
2. Bon Appetit
3. Tasty
4. Brothers Green Eats
5. Kenji Lopez-Alt
6. Laura in the Kitchen
7. You Suck at Cooking
8. Peaceful Cuisine

9. ChefSteps
10. Donal Skehan

Crafting: There is a vast crafting community on YouTube, so if you are a crafter, you will find others who share your passion. Whether you want to film tutorials or simply show off your craft supply hauls and projects, you will find an eager audience awaiting your content.

Beading, scrapbooking, knitting, quilting, card making, and any other type of crafting and DIY category can make for great videos, whether they are tutorials or hauls. Hauls from Hobby Lobby, Michael's, JoAnn, and even Dollar Tree can bring in a lot of views.

The crafting community on YouTube is huge, so be sure to connect with other crafters who are making videos by liking and commenting on their videos, too. I am not a crafter myself, but I have done well with some DIY Dollar Tree tutorials.

10 Popular Crafting Channels:

1. Innova Crafts
2. Isa's World
3. Origami with Jo Nakashima
4. Lia Griffith
5. aPasos Crafts DIY
6. Artkala
7. DIY Crafts TV
8. Shagufta Fyms
9. MASS Art and Craft
10. Stitch and Flower

Fashion: Do you love to put together outfits? Do you like to style clothing you find at thrift stores? Do you enjoy reviewing new fashion brands? Then a fashion-themed channel may be an excellent fit for you! Figure out your niche and expand on that. Maybe you have an eye for vintage or like to create looks based on designer duds. Or maybe you enjoy styling the different body types of your friends and family. Whatever your personal style or mantra is, there is an audience for it on YouTube.

Fashion influencers also share tips on closet organization, their jewelry collections, and try-on hauls from trending online brands. Body positivity and plus-size fashion are popular online trends as people want to embrace their bodies and learn what works best on their frames.

Signing up with Amazon and other affiliates will also allow you to link your looks and make money from referrals. You've likely seen "shop my look" links on social media posts of people showing off their outfits. These links are affiliate links, meaning the creator makes money when someone clicks through to the retailer and makes a purchase.

10 Popular Fashion Channels:

1. Tess Christine
2. Vanessa Ziletti
3. Jenn Im
4. Samantha Maria
5. Patricia Bright
6. Teaching Men's Fashion
7. Coolirpa
8. Kalyn Nicholson
9. Amber School
10. Summer Mckeen

Gaming: Video game channels are among the most popular on YouTube, with the top creators earning millions of dollars a year just by live-streaming themselves playing games. If you love to play video games, you can turn your hobby into income on YouTube.

Naturally, this will take a higher level of technology than simply filming on an iPhone, as you will be screen sharing your video game play next to a shot of you actually playing. But if you are already into playing video games, you likely already know how to stream that content on your computer and share it on YouTube.

10 Popular Gaming Channels:

1. LazerBeam
2. Markiplier
3. Jacksepticeye
4. PewDiePie
5. CoryxKenshin
6. VanossGaming
7. Dan TDM
8. PopularMMOs
9. H2ODelirious
10. The Game Theorists

Gardening: If you have a green thumb, consider sharing your gardening skills on YouTube. Many people want to learn about plants, flowers, and vegetable gardening. Prepping and off-grid living are becoming very popular topics on YouTube, and gardening fits in with those genres.

Share all your gardening information and watch your subscriber list (and AdSense money) grow along with your plants. Plus, with an Amazon Associates account, you can link the products you use and earn additional income.

10 Popular Gardening Channels:

1. Growing Your Greens
2. MIgardener
3. California Gardening
4. CaliKim29 Garden & Home DIY
5. Kitchen Gardening
6. Rob Bob's Backyard Farm & Aquaponics
7. Gardening Is My Passion
8. Garden Up
9. The Gardening Channel with James Prigioni
10. Run Gardening

Hauls & Subscription Boxes: Love to shop? Share your shopping hauls with your YouTube subscribers. Even a trip to the grocery store to stock the fridge can make for an exciting video. Trader Joe's and Costco hauls are wildly popular.

I film quite a few haul videos on my personal YouTube channel from stores such as Dollar Tree, Bath & Body Works, and Target, and they are always a big hit. Sometimes I even film "shop with me" videos and take my viewers along with me in vlog-style videos. Even grocery store hauls can bring in a large number of views.

Subscription boxes fall under the "Hauls" category, and this is something I cover extensively on my main YouTube channel. Subscription box companies offer themed boxes filled with everything from beauty products to home décor. Subscribers can get these boxes monthly or quarterly, depending on the service. And opening these boxes has become extremely popular on YouTube.

10 Popular Stores for Haul Videos:

1. Target
2. Dollar Tree
3. Costco
4. Walmart
5. Sam's Club
6. Costco
7. Trader Joe's
8. TJMaxx
9. Aldi
10. Big Lots

10 Popular Subscription Boxes

1. FabFitFun
2. Bespoke Post
3. Kiwi Crate by Kiwico
4. Lovevery

5. Ipsy
6. Stitch Fix
7. Rocksbox
8. BoxyCharm
9. Allure Beauty Box
10. Bath Bevy

Health & Fitness: Another hot YouTube channel theme is health, specifically diet and fitness. Whether it is nutrition or weight loss, bodybuilding, or running, many people turn to YouTube to get in shape. Natural food and specialty diets (gluten-free, vegan, raw) are also popular video topics.

10 Popular Health & Fitness Channels

1. Everyday Health
2. Health Tips
3. Kati Morton
4. Orange Health
5. Healthcare Triage
6. Live Healthy Life
7. Good Health 24/7
8. World Health Organization
9. Men's Health Magazines
10. High Intensity Health

How-To & Education: As I talked about in the filming equipment section, there are thousands of how-to videos on YouTube that cover nearly every topic you can think of, including how to film and edit YouTube videos. If there is an area or areas you are proficient in (computers, carpentry, crafting), creating how-to videos can be a great source of videos for your channel. Some channels are entirely dedicated to showing how to put together items purchased online.

I have recently relied on YouTube videos to show me how to build a shelf and to assemble a pressure washer, both of which I ordered on Amazon. Creators of these videos not only make money via AdSense but also from the affiliate links they provide.

For instance, in the video I watched on the pressure washer, the creator linked the pressure washer in the video's description box. The creator then earned an Amazon commission from anyone who clicked on the link and made a purchase on the site.

A bonus of reviewing products is that you will be contacted by many Amazon sellers who offer you a free product in exchange for you making a YouTube video about it. I have received free mattresses, pillows, vacuums, and small kitchen appliances from brands that simply want me to show their product in a video and give viewers the link to their websites.

10 Popular How-To Channels:

1. TED-Ed Lessons Worth Sharing
2. SmarterEveryDay
3. Vsauce
4. AsapSCIENCE
5. National Geographic
6. CrashCourse
7. Kurzgesagt
8. Scishow
9. Veritasium
10. Minutephysics

Lifehacks: If you like to scroll through social media, chances are you stumbled upon "lifehack" posts where people share shortcuts and tricks to do everything from peeling vegetables to packing a suitcase. The possibilities of how to present this content are endless.

You can film one hack per video or put together lists such as "Top 10 Ways to Save Money Eating Out." A search of "lists" on YouTube will bring up countless options. From "Top 10 List of Disney World Rides" to the "List of Top 15 Movies of All Time," there is a list for everything. It may not seem like riveting content, but a large audience is searching for it on YouTube.

10 Popular Lifehack Channels

1. Wengie
2. The King of Random
3. Natalies Outlet
4. Troom
5. Life Hacks & Experiments
6. DaveHax
7. Mr. Hacker
8. HawkGuruHacker
9. Life Hacks
10. Amazing Life Hacks Tricks

Mommy Videos: Are you a mom-to-be, or do you already have little ones in the home? There are many other mothers out there who you can connect with, whether by merely sharing your baby's milestones or talking about what you feed your toddler. Many women (and men!) want to interact with other parents online.

Homeschooling videos are also popular, as are baby and children's product reviews. Other videos that typically receive many views are kids' clothing hauls, back-to-school hauls, child-rearing tips, and what presents parents are buying their kids for the holidays.

10 Popular Mommy Channels:

1. WhatsUpMoms
2. Cute Girls Hairstyles
3. Team2Moms
4. Imomsohard
5. MOMables
6. Diary of an Indian Mom
7. Shelley Mummy Vlogs
8. Momhood and Beyond
9. Kids and Moms
10. Millennial Moms

Organization: Organizing is another hot YouTube channel theme. How to organize your house, office, car, kid's toys, crafts, garage, and basement can all make for great videos. If you excel at organizing, you may think there is no audience for this topic, but believe me, there are people out there who would love to watch you organize something as simple as a junk drawer! Organizing your home on a budget from dollar stores is something many people produce videos on, too.

And since Amazon is full of organizing products, an Amazon Associates account will allow you to link products your viewers can shop for. In fact, some creators only do videos with products purchased on Amazon to earn money from the affiliate links!

10 Popular Organizing Channels:

1. At Home with Nikki
2. Clutter Bug
3. Love Meg
4. The Organized Soprano
5. Dana K. White
6. Knight Designs
7. Mission 2 Organize
8. Suzanna Kaye Professional Organizer
9. Organized Mamas
10. Restore Order Professional Organizing

Restaurant & Food Reviews: If you are a foodie who loves to taste test the new dining and snack options in your area and when you travel, a channel dedicated to food reviews may be right up your alley. Whether you vlog while dining out, order fast food that you eat in your car, or do dedicated taste-testing videos at home, viewers gobble up food content!

10 Popular Food Review Channels:

1. Best Ever Food Review Show
2. TheReportOfTheWeek
3. Mark Wiens
4. Strictly Dumplin
5. Trevor James

6. The Food Ranger
7. Gary200
8. Delish
9. Timmy's Takeout
10. DFB Disney Food Blog

Reviews: Do you love to read or go to the movies? Are friends always asking you to recommend your favorite video games or CDs? Do you always buy the latest gadgets? Millions of people turn to YouTube for reviews, so if you love books, movies, television, video games, music, and/or electronics, consider making a channel where you offer your opinions!

If you review products, you will soon start to be contacted by companies offering to send you free items in exchange for video reviews. In recent years I have been sent a robotic vacuum, an air fryer, a humidifier, and numerous subscription boxes, all for free, just for showing them on my YouTube channel.

If you plan to do reviews, note that copyright issues will prevent you from using clips of movies, video games, television shows, or music. Still, you can hold up your own copy of a DVD or CD if you want some type of visual; or you can add still photos from the productions.

As I've noted several times, another way to make money on your channel, including for reviews, is to sign up for an Amazon Associates account and put your referral link in the description bar to the item you are reviewing. If someone buys something through your link, whether it is the item you reviewed or something else, you will earn a commission on their purchase.

10 Popular Review Channels:
1. Freakin' Reviews
2. Theneedledrop
3. TwinsthenewTrend
4. MovieIdol
5. Stop the FOMO

6. Digital Trends
7. Consumer Reports
8. The Try Guys
9. Grav3yardgirl
10. ThriftThick

Tags: Tags are trendy amongst YouTubers. Tags are simply question and answer lists, such as "50 Random Facts About Me." There are tags galore on YouTube, giving you an easy way to create content, as all you must do is answer the questions. Tags are especially helpful if you are just starting on YouTube and unsure of what kinds of videos you want to make.

For a complete list of tags, check out my book, *The Big Book of YouTube Tags: Dozens of Fun Quizzes & Questionnaires for Video Creators,* which is available on Amazon.

Thrifting: Are you a bargain hunter who loves to score the racks at Goodwill for the best deals? Do you spend your Saturday mornings driving around town in search of garage sales? If you love to thrift, an audience is waiting for you on YouTube! From shop-with-me vlogs to hauls and even DIY refurbishment of secondhand furniture, thrifting is a hot topic with an eager audience on YouTube.

As someone who thrifts to sell on Ebay, there is also a large reselling community on YouTube. Creators all of ages and from all over America film videos of their hauls to sell on sites like Ebay and Poshmark, along with sharing tips about the reselling business.

10 Popular Thrifting Channels:

1. Paul Cantu
2. Coolirpu
3. itsHardin
4. Threads Obsessed
5. Thrifted Living
6. ThriftersAnonymous

7. Gentle Thrifty Mama
8. Ms fili
9. Mrs. Shopalot
10. There She Goes

Travel: Do you love to travel? Perhaps you take frequent road trips or cruises, or maybe you are an RV or camping enthusiast. Many YouTube viewers would love to see your travel footage, including your packing tips, dining recommendations, and money-saving advice.

I have filmed many Walt Disney Vacation vlogs for my YouTube channel over the years, and they are always a big hit. Cruise vlogs are also extremely popular on YouTube.

10 Popular Travel Channels:

1. TFIL
2. Wil Dasovich
3. Lost LeBlanc
4. High On Life
5. Adam the Woo
6. Tim Tracker
7. Expedia
8. Erik Conover
9. Flying the Nest
10. Share with Wonder

Vlogging: People worldwide chronicle their lives through vlogs, many doing so daily. Note that vlogging is very time-consuming and can feel like an invasion of privacy if you are not careful; however, many folks are earning a part-time and even a full-time income on YouTube by sharing 10-to-20-minute snippets of their daily lives. Note that you do not have to be a daily vlogger to have a vlog channel; you can film as many or as few vlogs as you would like, although it helps stick to a schedule, such as posting vlogs three times a week.

Suppose you enjoy vlogging but do not want to commit to a set vlogging schedule. In that case, you can simply vlog whenever you are doing something particularly exciting or during a "vlogging month" such as "Vlogmas" (vlogging for Christmas), "Vlogtober" (vlogging every day in October), "VEDA" (vlogging every day in April), or "Vlogust" (vlogging every day in August). I, myself, have done "Vlogust," "Vlogtober," and "Vlogmas" in the past.

The hard part about vlogging for me has been that the subscribers who love vlogs REALLY love vlogs and desperately want them to continue daily. It is a lot of pressure to keep up with daily uploads. For me, another downside to vlogging is that you are exposing yourself to more criticism and scrutiny than a regular sit-down or one-topic video might bring. Even when you only show 10-minutes out of a 24-hour day, viewers start to assume that they know everything about you and can either be overly friendly (i.e., a bit like a stalker!) or too critical.

Most daily vloggers start out interacting with viewers in the comments but stop doing so as their subscribers increase because they feel the need to guard their privacy more closely. If vlogging interests you, consider starting by doing it once a week. You can always expand to more frequent vlogs if you decide you really enjoy doing them and do not feel like you are exposing too much of your personal life.

10 Popular Vlogging Channels:
1. Casey Neistat
2. RomanAtwoodVlogs
3. Nas Daily
4. Morgans Vlogs
5. Mr. Ben Brown
6. FunForLouis
7. Emma Chamberlain
8. Sacconejolys
9. Ryland Vlogs
10. Michel Janse

CHAPTER FIVE: HOW TO EARN MONEY ON YOUTUBE

So far, in this book, I have already discussed how you make money on YouTube via AdSense; but there are other ways you can bring in even more income with your videos. While AdSense will be your first money-making stream, it will likely not be your last as you grow your channel.

In fact, the largest YouTube channels make most of their money from sources other than AdSense. For example, YouTuber Jeffree Star referred to his AdSense money as "extra" income on top of his beauty empire! And while you may not reach the level of fortune that Star has, you still have the potential to earn money on YouTube.

ADSENSE: At the beginning of this book, I covered the basics for monetizing your videos with AdSense, which you do as part of the YouTube Partner Program. But you must understand how AdSense works and how you can best utilize it on your channel to maximize your earnings.

AdSense is the route by which Google sells advertising. You have likely seen Google-branded pop-up ads on various websites. The money that advertisers pay for those ads is processed through AdSense. When you are monetized on YouTube, Google will run ads on your videos; just like ads that appear on text-based websites, the ads that appear on videos are purchased and sold through AdSense. You can think of Google Ads and AdSense as being one and the same.

Whether on a website or in a YouTube video, the Google ads shown to you have matched the content you are reading or watching. For instance, if you are reading a travel article, you will likely see ads for Disney World or the various cruise lines.

The same is true for the YouTube videos you watch. These ads are created and paid for by advertising companies. These companies pay Google to run the ads, and Google then splits the money with the content creators, both on blogs and websites as well as on YouTube. If you are creating beauty videos, then logically, the makeup companies that run Google ads will be interested in placing their ads on your videos.

How much you will earn via Google AdSense depends on several different factors, such as the type of ads placed on your videos, how viewers respond to the ads, and the cost that each particular advertiser is paying Google to run their ads. The more a brand pays for an ad, the more you will make if people watch your video.

On YouTube, how much money a video makes is first determined by the **CPM**. CPM stands for **cost per 1,000 impressions**, and the CPM is what YouTube can charge advertisers for ads placed on your videos. While you are not paid the CPM amount, it is essential to determine your **RPM**, which is your revenue cut.

Again, **CPM stands for what Google charges advertisers**, and **RPM is what Google pays you**.

CPMs can be as low as 50 cents and as high as hundreds of dollars per one thousand views; it all depends on the video's content.

Remember, the CPM is the amount of money YouTube charges advertisers, not the amount you are paid. Your RPM is usually half of your CPM, so a high CPM typically results in a high RPM.

As a YouTube creator, you are paid per 1,000 views on all your videos combined throughout the month. For example, my general lifestyle videos earn around $12 CPM per 1,000 views. However, on average, my reselling videos earn $35 CPM per 1,000 views.

Why the difference? Well, lifestyle videos are a dime a dozen on YouTube; there is so much competition in this category that content creators end up splitting the share of advertising between thousands of different channels. However, reselling is a tiny, niche category, but one with a loyal viewer base. And it is an audience that is specifically interested in money-making opportunities.

While finance companies will not find their audience on makeup tutorial videos, they will find them on videos about Ebay and Poshmark. Therefore, Google can charge those advertisers more as their audience is small. And since the reselling community on YouTube is relatively small, those of us who make reselling videos split the advertising dollars with fewer creators, making our CPMs higher. While there are hundreds of thousands of makeup tutorial videos, there may be less than 100 videos about how to list items for sale on Poshmark.

Bottom line: Niche content may not get as many views, but the advertising rates tend to be much higher, meaning your chances of earning money with a small audience are also much higher. Niche categories are also easier to break into. There are tens of thousands of gaming channels but not as many business channels. Even if your content falls under one of the larger categories, try to niche it down by homing in on a specific topic.

For example, maybe you would focus on baking instead of a general cooking channel. Or rather than crafting, you would produce videos related to one specific crafting method, such as jewelry making.

I have been fortunate that my CPMs have been on the higher side throughout my YouTube career. The average CPM across YouTube is only $4 per 1,000 views. However, this rate varies between every channel and can vary daily. My CPMs are constantly changing, going up and down depending on the money advertisers are investing in YouTube ads for the videos I make.

Once your YouTube videos are monetized to earn AdSense revenue, you can track your CPM in your account's **YouTube Studio** area. Simply click on the **Analytics** tab on the left side of the page to see your AdSense totals (you can customize the date range), and then click on **Revenue** to see your CPM. I personally like to check my numbers once a week to see how my month is going.

However, while your CPM number is important, it is your RPM, which stands for **Revenue Per Mile**, which is the amount of money you are actually earning. This metric represents how much money YouTube is paying you per 1,000 video views via Ads, Channel Memberships, YouTube Premium revenue, Super Chats, and Super Stickers (I will discuss each of these further along in this chapter).

CPM is the cost per 1000 ad impressions BEFORE YouTube takes its cut.

RPM is your total revenue per 1000 views AFTER YouTube takes its cut.

When I look at my analytics on YouTube, the number I home in on is my RPM, as that is what YouTube is paying me for every 1,000 views. However, it's important to remember that your CPM and RPM fluctuate almost daily. Therefore, you want to focus on your average numbers.

While your CPM is an advertiser-focused metric that only

includes income from the monetized ads on your videos, RPM is a creator-focused metric that provides for total revenue reported from all available sources. It also includes the total number of views from your videos. Your RPM number will always be lower than your CPM number as it is calculated after YouTube's revenue share and because it includes all views, even those on videos that, for whatever reason, were not monetized.

Confused? Do not worry; most people are! Google is data-driven and gives YouTube creators a lot of numbers.

To be honest, I myself rarely dig too deeply into these numbers. I focus on tracking my revenue share in the **YouTube Studio section** of my YouTube account (simply click on your profile picture on the top right-hand side of your YouTube account and select *YouTube Studio* from the menu to find yours). By clicking on the **Analytics** icon on the left-hand side of the page, you can bring up your **Channel Analytics**. From here, you can see your current revenue and several other statistics. You can also choose the date range, including:

- Last seven days
- Last 28 days
- Last 90 days
- Last 365 days
- Lifetime
- Current year
- Previous year
- Each of the past three months
- Custom

As I mentioned earlier, I personally narrow my display screen to the current month to see how my revenue is tracking for that particular month. Selecting any of the time options will narrow down your statistics on an overview page where you can see your **Views, Watch time (hours), New subscribers,** and **Estimated revenue.**

I like to narrow down my numbers by clicking on the **Revenue** tab to see my RPM and CPM. Through red arrows, YouTube will also show you whether your numbers are up or down from the previous time frame. My running tally of revenue for the month lets me know how I am doing and maybe where I need to improve.

That being said, it's important to note that the reporting of these numbers does lag a bit. You will need to wait until the end of the month when YouTube finalizes your revenue report to see what you actually earned. Sometimes the number I see at the end of the month is higher when I get paid. However, I still like to check my numbers to get an idea of where I am.

Further down the page under **Revenue** are even more helpful insights and statistics, including your estimated revenue for each of the past six months, along with your top-performing videos via revenue for the current month. Noting your top-performing videos will show you what type of content your audience is reacting to, which will help you decide what videos to produce in the future.

You can also access your **Reach statistics,** such as impressions, clicks-through rates, views, and unique views. Under **Engagement**, you will find your watch time in hours and your average view duration. And finally, under **Audience**, you can see your unique viewers, average views per viewer, and the number of new subscribers.

Your subscriber count will go up and down, some days more than others. People are constantly leaving YouTube while new people are joining. And some people unsubscribe and resubscribe to channels regularly. You just hope that your numbers increase faster than they decrease.

All of these numbers, percentages, and statistics can be overwhelming. But the good thing is that you do not have to pay attention to them unless you enjoy digging through data. As I said, I only focus on my current running revenue balance and my CPM and RPM. And in truth, it is only my RPM number and my running total of AdSense that is of any importance, as that is how much money I will be paid. And when it's all said and done, the only real number that matters are the amount deposited into my bank account.

Oh, and when does YouTube pay you? **Once you have earned at least $100 via Google AdSense, Google will initiate a payment to you the following month.** So, if you earn $100 or more in January, you will get paid your January AdSense revenue in February, typically during the third week of the month. The money will carry over to the next month if you don't earn enough monthly to qualify for a payout. So, if you earned $50 in January, that $50 would carry into February. If you earned $60 in February, your total would then be $110, which you would receive in April.

You can choose to have your money directly deposited into your bank account. Or, for a fee, you can have Google mail you a check. I choose direct deposit as it is automatic and so much easier than waiting on a paper check that I then have to take to the bank.

Remember that **if you earn $600 or more from AdSense in a year, YouTube will provide you with a 1099 form** to submit with your taxes. YouTube will notify you if you have a tax form available, which you can then print out from your Google AdSense account page. I will be going over YouTube accounting in the next chapter.

AFFILIATE LINKS: While AdSense is the primary way most people earn money on YouTube, another way to bring in cash from your videos is through affiliate links. When you sign up to be an affiliate with a company, you can access affiliate links that will pay you a commission whenever someone buys an item through your personal link.

Amazon offers the most popular referral program, which I've already referenced numerous times, called **Amazon Associate**, which many YouTubers use, as well as bloggers and social media influencers. I have been an *Amazon Associate* even before starting my YouTube channel, as I would share my link via my other social media accounts. I then utilized the program on my blog. And today, I use the program in a Facebook group I have devoted to deals and freebies, as well as on my business Facebook page and on Twitter.

By signing up as an *Amazon Associate*, you can create referral links to any of the products on Amazon's website. Then if you use or mention a product in your video and provide a link to it in your YouTube video description box, you will earn a commission if anyone goes through your link to purchase that product. If you show anything in your video that can be purchased on Amazon, you will want to link it underneath your video.

However, it is important to note that the person who clicks on your link does not have to purchase the exact product you link to; you will earn a commission on ANY items they buy once they are on Amazon's site if they got there using your referral link.

Let's say you link a teapot that you showed in your video, and someone clicks on it; they don't have to buy the teapot. Amazon will track all their purchases over the next 24 hours, crediting you with anything they buy. One year I made several hundred dollars as people used my *Amazon Associates* links to buy new televisions during the holidays. I didn't even link to any televisions!

With Amazon being the largest e-commerce site globally, it makes sense that most YouTube creators are also *Amazon Associates*, as it is an easy way to earn additional money. Go to any large YouTube channel. You will likely find several *Amazon Associate* links in the description boxes below their videos, most often for the equipment, they are using to film their videos. Those $1000 DSRL cameras can earn you a hefty *Amazon Associate* commission if you link yours under your videos!

The first link under my videos is to my Amazon storefront; a perk offered when you have 10,000 YouTube subscribers.

This unique "influencer" *Amazon Associate* storefront gives me a dedicated page on Amazon where I can organize all of the products I offer. In addition to the books, I write under my own name, I also create journals, planners, and notebooks that I sell on Amazon under the "Jean Lee" publishing name. Plus, I have a section for the reselling supplies I use and a section for the home products I often show in my vlogs.

I can easily direct viewers to this one link if they want to check out my books and other items. And I can quickly delete or add new items at any time.

To sign up for an Amazon Affiliate account, visit affiliate-program.amazon.com.

In addition to the *Amazon Associate* program, there are all kinds of companies that offer affiliate opportunities. In addition to Amazon, you can sign up for FREE to be an affiliate with:

Adobe: Apply at adobe.com/affiliates.html. The Adobe Affiliate Program allows you to earn commissions when you promote Adobe Creative Cloud, Adobe Stock, and Adobe Document Cloud on your website, blog, or social media channels.

Audible: Apply at audible.com/ep/affiliate-intro. Earn advertising fees when you refer viewers to qualifying Audible products and memberships.

Brandcycle: Apply at brandcycle.com/. Brandcycle allows influencers to partner with over 400 retail brands to access premium commission rates and exclusive offers.

Ebay Partner Network: Apply at partnernetwork.ebay.com/. Earn money by driving traffic and promoting sales across Ebay.

Honey: joinhoney.com/business/get-started. Earn money through this money-saving browser extension.

Movavi: Apply at movavi.com/partners/affiliate-program/. Earn money promoting the Movavi video software.

Rakuten (formerly LinkShare): Apply at

rakutenadvertising.com/affiliate/. Work with the top brands across industries.

Rakuten also has a shopping portal, formerly called Ebates, that pays users a percentage back on their purchases. Shoppers simply create a free Rakuten account and search the site for the retailer they want to shop from. They then click through to the store's website via Rakuten's link.

Rakuten automatically tracks their spending, giving them a percentage back of their total purchase amount (anywhere from 1% up to 20%, depending on the site). Every three months, Rakuten automatically mails users out rebate checks. There are no points to track or special codes to enter; the entire process is automated on Rakuten's end.

While I use Rakuten for my shopping rebates, I also use their affiliate program to make money. When you sign up for a Rakuten account, you are also given your own affiliate link to share on social media, including on YouTube. When someone signs up for Rakuten using your affiliate link and makes a purchase, you then earn $25.

Any affiliate income you make from Rakuten is added to your rebate total, and a check is mailed out to you every three months. It is a safe, easy, and effective program to increase your overall YouTube earnings. And it is why you will see Rakuten affiliate links in many YouTube description boxes.

Shopify: Apply at shopify.com/affiliates. Earn commissions through your own Shopify store or by promoting others.

Sellfy: Apply at sellfy.com/affiliates/. Earn commissions by bringing customers to the Sellfy website.

ShareASale: Apply at shareasale.com/info/. Earn money by promoting partner offers and brands.

ShopHer Media: Apply at shophermedia.com/partners/. Earn commissions by directing shoppers to the various ShopHer brands.

ShopStyle Collective: Apply at shopstylecollective.com/. Earn money by sharing links to products you love. ShopStyle has thousands of brands available to promote.

Skillshare: Apply at skillshare.com/affiliates. Earn $7 for every new customer you refer to Skillshare, a website that hosts online classes and video lessons.

Skimlinks: Apply at skimlinks.com/. Skimlinks has a global network of 48,500 merchants from which you can earn commissions.

TripAdvisor: Apply at tripadvisor.com/affiliates. Partner with the world's largest travel site to earn 50% commissions for providing hotel booking links.

Twitch: Apply at affiliate.twitch.tv/. Twitch is an affiliate network specifically targeted toward streaming content.

REFERRAL LINKS: While affiliate programs pay you in cash, referral programs reward you with products or credits for paying for your purchases. For example, for a while, I subscribed to numerous subscription boxes, which I reviewed on my channel. If the company had a referral link, I would provide the link in the video's description box. Then, I earned rewards if someone signed up for the subscription using my link. Sometimes it was points toward free products; other times, it was free boxes or products.

Since affiliate programs pay in cash, I generally prefer them over referral links. However, some companies offer both; it is then up to me to decide which reward is better. In some cases, I use the affiliate link to earn cash; in other cases, I may use the referral link to earn free products. It all depends on the reward.

For instance, I have a subscription to Grove Collaborative, a membership-based website selling eco-friendly household products. They have both an affiliate program and a referral program. I choose to use my referral link to use the credits toward buying my own cleaning supplies. For me, the credits are more valuable than the affiliate money I could earn, even though the affiliate percentage is higher than the referral credit.

Nowadays, nearly every brand and service offers a referral program, including major airlines and hotels, clothing and beauty companies, subscription boxes, and membership services. I belong to numerous referral programs, including FabFitFun, Causebox, and Thrive Marketplace, to name a few.

Whenever you show an item of yours in a video, say a piece of clothing or a kitchen accessory, visit the brand's website to see if they offer an affiliate or referral program so that when you link the product in your video, you will have the potential to earn either cash or credit. If you have a blog or website, you can also put ads from these companies on your site to earn credits and free products that way.

Some popular referral programs are as follows. A simple Google search for each company name followed by "referral program" will take you directly to the pages to sign up. You may find that some will lead you to the affiliate programs listed in the previous section, but some will have their own dedicated program.

Acorns: This financial investment service specializes in micro-investing and robo-investing. Customers and those they refer receive a $5 bonus upon successfully setting up an account.

Airbnb: Earn up to $30 in credits when you refer someone who completes a reservation as a guest or a host.

Alaska Airlines: Earn bonus miles when your referrals sign up and are approved for the Alaska Airlines Visa Signature Card.

American Express: If you have an American Express account, you can earn Membership Rewards for every successful referral.

American Giant: American Giant's tagline is "best hoodies in the world." Customers who successfully refer friends earn $20, while the referrals get a 15% discount.

Amerisleep: This natural memory foam mattress company will reward you with a prepaid Visa gift card when referrals order a mattress through your link.

Backcountry: This outdoor clothing seller offers both you and your referrals $10 toward future purchases.

Birchbox: Birchbox is the original beauty subscription box. Their referral program offers customers 100 Birchbox Points ($10) when someone signs up using their link. The referrals receive $9 off their first box with a minimum 3-month membership.

Blinds.com: This custom window treatment retailer gives both the referrer and the referral recipient $20 on all orders.

Blue Bottle Coffee: This coffee supplier gives customers and referrals $20 in credit toward future purchases for every order.

Boden: This clothing retailer has a large online presence. You can earn a $15 credit when someone purchases through your link. The referral will receive 20% off their first purchase.

Brooklinen: This sheet and linen company offers several ways to earn credit, such as following them on social media and leaving reviews. Customers and referrals each receive 25% off their purchase of $100 or more.

BurnCycle: BurnCycle offers indoor cycling classes in Oregon and Washington. If you have one of these gyms near you, you can earn 15% when you successfully refer five people to complete a spin class. The people you refer get 15% off their next month's membership fee or class package.

Canva: This popular digital graphic design site gives customers credits toward premium images when their referral creates an account and completes a design.

Casper: Casper is an online mattress company that offers a rotating offering of referral credit offers, such as Amazon gift cards. The referred customer receives 20% off their order.

Chase: Chase offers online banking and credit cards. Users can earn between 5,000 and 10,000 points (equal to $50 and $100, respectively) when they refer friends and family.

Choice Hotels: Earn points toward future hotel stays when referrals complete a stay with a participating hotel.

Coinbase: You can earn $10 worth of Bitcoin for everyone you refer.

Discover: Both customers and those they refer can earn statement credits via their referral program.

Dropbox: This online data storage service upgrades customers' storage for every referral they make.

eBags: This online luggage store gives customers $10 in reward points for every referral. Referrals get 65% off their first order.

Everlane: This online clothing retailer gives customers $25 credit for every successful referral.

FabFitFun: As I mentioned earlier, I subscribe to the FabFitFun subscription box, which means I am given referral codes to share. I earn $15 in referral credits for everyone who signs up using my link. The referrals receive $10 off their first box.

Fabletics: This Kate Hudson-founded company offers a fitness wear subscription. Subscribers are given a referral link that gives new customers 50% off their first order. For every friend you refer, you earn $10 in-store credit.

Farm Fresh To You: This organic fruit and vegetable delivery service give customers a unique Refer-A-Friend link to share that gives referrals $15 toward their first order. In return, you receive a $25 credit.

Getaround: Called the Airbnb of car sharing, referral users earn $20 credit for anyone who signs up using their link.

Girlfriend Collective: This activewear brand sells clothes from recycled materials and offers a pair of free leggings when someone uses your referral link to make a purchase. The referrals are given $10 off their purchase of $95 or more.

Glossier: This online cosmetics company awards you with $10 in-store credit when a referred customer clicks on your link, creates an account and places an order. The referrals receive 10% off their first purchase.

Groupon: Groupon is a deal site that offers discounts on products and services, both online and locally. Users can earn $10 in Groupon Bucks for every referral that purchases a Groupon.

Hanna Anderson: This children's apparel company gives customers 20% off a future order when referring friends and family. Referrals receive 20% off their first order.

HelloFresh: This meal subscription service rewards customers with a $20 credit for every successful referral. The referral gets $40 off their first box.

HotelTonight: Earn money toward your next booking when you share your referral link.

Hunter: Hunter makes pricey boots and outerwear. You can earn $15 per referral when they make a purchase. The referral gets $15 off their first order.

Intuit QuickBooks: Earn a $100 pre-paid Visa card for every person who subscribes through your link.

Lime Lush Boutique: This online women's clothing shop offers you $20 in-store credit for every successful referral. The referral gets 20% off their first order.

Lyft: Another popular ridesharing program, Lyft rewards when someone uses their referral link. You can choose cash, Lyft credit, or a combination of the two.

Madison Reed: This hair care company has a "share the love" program where you can earn a $15 credit for every referral that signs up using your link. The referrals receive a $15 discount on their first purchase.

Marriott Hotel: Earn up to 50,000 bonus points when you refer up to five new customers per year.

MeUndies: This online underwear shop rewards you with $20 in credit for each successful referral. Referrals get 20% off their first purchase.

Minted: This online stationery company offers users $25 in credit when someone they refer purchases $100 or more. The referral also receives $25 off their first order.

Moo: This online print and design company offers two ways to earn rewards through referrals. When you refer a friend, they have the potential to win a $20 gift card. If you refer a business with a minimum of 10 employees, the reward increases to $150. The referrals themselves get 24% off their first order.

Naturebox: An online healthy snack shop that rewards customers with $10 off future orders for every friend they refer. Your referral link offers people 50% off their first order.

Outdoor Voices: Earn $20 to spend at this activewear retailer for every referral who signs up. The people you refer get 20% off their first order.

Peapod: This online grocery store allows you to share your referral link on social media or via email. Your link offers people $50 off their first two orders. In return, you will receive $25 toward your next order.

Rebecca Minkoff: This luxury women's retailer has a Refer-A-Friend program that gives both you and the referral $20 for each successful referral.

Robinhood: This online investment app rewards you and your referrals with free stock of up to $500 a calendar year.

Quip: Quip is a subscription-based dental company that provides customers with electric toothbrushes, refill packs, toothpaste, and dental floss. Earn $5 in credits for every referral you make. The referrals also earn $5 credit for every successful purchase they make. Quip also rewards you with $5 in credit when you invite your dentist to join.

Seated: This restaurant reservation app gives customers and those they refer credits to apply toward future reservations. When you have five successful referrals, you will be upgraded to "Seated Partner," where you can earn bonus rewards.

Shoes for Crews: This online store sells slip-resistant footwear to the workforce. Referrals reward both individuals with a $10 credit.

Shyp: This online shipping and fulfillment company serves e-commerce stores and small businesses with brick-and-mortar locations. Users can earn credit toward future shipments when they share their referral code.

Soylent: Soylent is a meal-replacement product. Their refer-a-friend program rewards you in points when referrals spend $24 or more on their first subscription order. Points can be redeemed on your own purchases. Referrals receive $10 off their first subscription of $24 or more.

Swagbucks: One of the first points-based rewards companies offers customers gift cards and cash for completing activities online. Their referral program awards you 10% of whatever your referrals earn.

Thinx: This online retailer has a strong focus on women's health. Customers receive $10 for every customer they refer, and referrals are given $10 off their first order.

Timberland: Timberland sells rugged shoes and boots. You can earn 20% off your future purchase when someone you refer makes a purchase. The referrals also receive 20% off their first order.

Uber: The popular ride-share company rewards you with

discounts and free rides when people sign up using your link.

Uniglo: This Japan-based clothing retailer gives customers $10 for every successful referral. The referrals receive $10 off their first order.

Vera Bradley: Vera Bradley specializes in bags in fun prints. Their Refer-A-Friend program rewards both you and the referral with 20% off a future purchase.

Verizon: If you are a Verizon customer, you can utilize their Refer-A-Friend program to earn up to $100 on a prepaid Mastercard when you successfully refer a new customer.

Vistaprint: This online print company sells various custom stationery products. Customers receive $10 when they successfully refer a new customer.

Vonage: Vonage is a "voice over internet protocol" service provider. Customers earn a $50 gift card for every referral who signs up for their service.

Winc: An online wine subscription service gives you two complimentary bottles of wine when anyone uses your link to place an order. The referral will also receive $22 of wine with their first purchase.

SPONSORSHIPS: In addition to earning money through AdSense, Amazon Associates, Rakuten, affiliate links, and referral links, you can also bring in cash through sponsorships. A sponsorship is when a company pays you to film a video. If a company has a product to promote, they will send you the item and pay you to film a video about it. If it is a service, the company will pay you to talk about their company.

A major cosmetic brand sponsored me a couple of years ago. They sent me a box of their makeup to review, and I filmed a video of me testing it out. On top of giving me free products, they also paid me a sponsorship fee. Note that you need to disclose sponsored videos, both verbally within the video and in the video's description box.

The more subscribers a channel has, the more lucrative sponsorships can be. Many large YouTube channels make more money from sponsorships than they do from AdSense. It takes a while to build up a large enough audience to attract sponsors; I began receiving sponsorship offers when my channel hit 5,000 subscribers (although I started getting offers of free products when my second channel barely had 1,000 subscribers). But it depends on what kind of content you are producing and how many actual views your videos typically get. Most brands will judge your channel based on your videos' average views, not necessarily by your subscriber numbers.

While most sponsorships come from companies contacting creators directly, you can also sign up with sponsorship companies to connect you with potential sponsors. These companies include, but are not limited to:

AspireIQ: Formerly called Revfluence, AspireIQ markets itself as the leading influencer marketing platform. They connect brands with influencers, paying creators to create content that drives traffic to the companies they represent, including Bed Bath & Beyond, Marriott, Walmart, and Nike. In addition to YouTube, you can also earn money from them on your blog/website, Facebook page, Twitter feed, and even Pinterest. Learn more at aspireiq.com.

Channel Pages by FanBridge: Channel Pages has no minimum YouTube subscriber count to qualify for signing up. They have an extensive collection of brands, both big and small. Their platform lets you connect with brands and apply for collaboration opportunities with other channels. Learn more at channelpages.com.

Content BLVD: Content BLVD works with cosmetics brands such as Urban Decay and Skin & Co. Content BLVD works exclusively with YouTubers who are paid to review the brands they represent. Not only can you get free products, but you will also be paid to make a video about them. Learn more at contentblvd.com.

Grapevine: Grapevine works with influencers with 10,000 YouTube subscribers or 10,000 Instagram followers. However, even if you haven't reached that level of followers, you can still sign up with them. They help you choose brand deals based on your channel size, niche, and demographics. Some companies they work with are Walgreens, NYX, and Remington. Learn more at grapevinevillage.com.

Izea: There are no minimum subscriber counts in order to sign up with Izea, a company that works to connect food, fashion, beauty, and lifestyle brands with content creators. Some of the companies they represent include Subway, Levi's, and Ebay. They also offer freelancing gigs. Learn more at izea.com.

TapInfluence: TapInfluence has no minimum subscriber requirement and can connect you with food, fashion, beauty, and lifestyle brands such as WhiteWave Food, MtoM Consulting, and Stella & Chewy's. Their "open bidding" feature lets you bid on projects that match your content. Learn more at tapinfluence.com.

YouTube Brand Connect: Formerly called Famebit, the newly rebranded YouTube Brand Connect offers YouTube creators sponsorships for big brands, including Canon, Sony, and Adidas. YouTube Brand Connect is currently invite-only for channels with 25,000 subscribers. If you become eligible, YouTube will notify you within your YouTube Studio interface.

Note that the companies listed above are not the only places to obtain sponsorships, as some brands work independently to connect with creators. Once you start gaining subscribers, you will likely start to be contacted directly by companies who either want to send you free products to review or who are willing to pay you a sponsorship fee for mention in a video.

A critical part of sponsorships is settling on the amount of money you expect to be paid. If you are just starting out on YouTube, you cannot expect a company to pay you thousands of dollars to sponsor a video. In fact, in the early days of your YouTube career, you may only be able to film videos in exchange for free products.

However, as your channel grows, you can start to expect payment for your services. Most brands will try to pay you as little as possible, if anything at all, so, you must go into YouTube with the mindset that your time is valuable. If a company approaches you with a sponsorship offer, it is because they feel you are a good fit for their brand. Therefore, they should already expect that they will need to pay you to film a sponsored video for them.

While sponsors look at your total subscriber count, they also examine how many views your videos average. Only you can answer how much you will be comfortable charging, although a good formula to start with is $0.05 to $0.15 per view or $50 to $150 per 1,000 views. Some brands ask you for your rate, while others propose a fixed price. In the end, only you can decide the rate you will charge.

You must have policies in place before accepting a sponsorship deal. You want to agree on:

1. When will the video go live?
2. How long will the video need to be in terms of length?
3. Does the brand need to approve the video before it launches?
4. When and how will you receive your payment?
5. Will the company be providing you with a script?
6. Will the company provide links and discount codes to share with your viewers?
7. Will you be given free products to show in your video?
8. What else does the company expect from you? For example, will you be expected to share the video on social media?

9. Will the company require that you use specific hashtags?
10. Will the company provide disclosure text in the video's description box?

Some companies will ask very little of you other than filming a video discussing their product or service, while others will expect you to sign a contract and complete numerous steps to get paid. I have had some brands mail me a product to show in a video, while others have demanded I sign a contract with detailed instructions on how, what, where, and when to film. The more a company expects of you, the more you should expect from them in terms of compensation.

SELLING YOUR OWN PRODUCTS: From tee shirts and coffee mugs to courses and books, YouTube creators frequently sell their own merchandise, also called "merch." My YouTube channel drives traffic to my books (in addition to this book, I have written several books about selling on Ebay and making money online), my Etsy shop, my Ebay store, and print-on-demand items that I sell, both on Amazon and TeePublic.

I provide links to all my products in the description boxes below every video I post, hoping that some of my viewers will purchase my products. I do not think I would be as successful as I have been with my books if it was not for YouTube driving traffic to them and subscribers buying them.

Creating your own merchandise is easy on sites like TeePublic and TeeSpring. I create my designs using Canva Pro software, which requires a small monthly fee. An app like WordSwag is free and easy to use for text-only designs. Or sites like Vecteezy and Creative Fabric offer subscriptions to access graphics you can use for commercial use.

I have a TeePublic store that is linked under my YouTube videos, and I sell items ranging from tee shirts to coffee mugs there every week. I also have merchandise I created in TeeSpring that appears below my videos. The TeeSpring offerings directly collaborate with YouTube, hence the links under the videos.

If you have a nickname or tagline, consider slapping it on a tee shirt or coffee mug and offering it up for sale to your YouTube viewers to help grow your brand and bring in extra money. I have friends who create new merchandise for every season. The TeeSpring option connected to your YouTube account makes adding merch easy. All you then do is collect your share of the profits.

CHANNEL MEMBERSHIPS: Channel memberships are a relatively new feature for YouTube creators. Memberships allow viewers to join your channel through monthly payments, enabling them to receive benefits such as special emojis, badges, stickers, and videos only offered to members.

Note that there is a minimum eligibility requirement that creators must meet before being able even to apply to offer Channel Memberships. As of this writing, requirements include:

- Your channel must have more than 1,000 subscribers
- Your channel must be enrolled in the YouTube Partner Program
- You must be over 18 years of age
- You must be located in one of the eligible countries (Argentina, Australia, Austria, Bahrain, Belarus, Belgium, Bolivia, Bosnia and Herzegovina, Brazil, Bulgaria, Canada, Chile, Colombia, Costa Rica, Croatia, Cyprus, Czech Republic, Denmark, Dominican Republic, Ecuador, El Salvador, Estonia, Finland, France, Germany, Greece, Guatemala, Honduras, Hong Kong, Hungary, Iceland, India, Indonesia, Ireland, Israel, Italy, Japan, Kuwait, Latvia, Lebanon, Liechtenstein, Lithuania, Luxembourg, Macedonia, Malaysia, Malta, Mexico, Netherlands, New Zealand, Nicaragua, Norway, Oman, Panama, Paraguay, Peru, Philippines, Poland, Portugal, Qatar, Romania, Russia, Saudi Arabia, Senegal, Serbia, Singapore, Slovakia,

Slovenia, South Africa, South Korea, Spain, Sweden, Switzerland, Taiwan, Thailand, Turkey, Uganda, United Arab Emirates, United Kingdom, United States, Uruguay, Vietnam)
- Your channel has a Community Tab
- Your channel is not set as "made for kids"
- Your channel does not have a significant number of ineligible videos (such as set as being "made for kids" or with music claims)
- You are complying with YouTube's terms and policies

If you are eligible and choose to offer Channel Memberships to your viewers, you can select from several "perks" to features, including:

- Badges
- Emojis
- Private videos
- Live chats
- Downloads of content
- In-person meetings
- Contests
- Sweepstakes

Some creators also offer physical items they mail out to their channel members, such as stickers, cards, shirts, and more. You can offer memberships priced as low as $0.99 per month up to $99.99 a month. Creators receive 70% of membership revenue after applicable taxes, and fees are taken out.

YOUTUBE PREMIUM: YouTube Premium is a subscription service that costs $11.99 per month and allows viewers to:

- Watch videos ad-free
- Download videos to watch offline
- Play videos in the background while using other apps
- Access the YouTube Music App
- Listen to music ad-free
- Download music to listen to offline

- Play music in the background while using other apps
- Watch ad-free YouTube Kids videos as well as the ability to play offline
- Listen to Google Play Music (for most countries)

Creators do not have to subscribe to YouTube Premium for their videos to be included in the subscription. And while ads will not appear on your videos if someone with a YouTube Premium account is viewing them, you will still receive a cut of the membership fees that are being paid to YouTube by subscribed viewers.

SUPER CHATS & SUPER STICKERS: Super Chats and Super Stickers allow viewers to connect with creators during live chats. Viewers can purchase Super Chats to send creators money; their comment then appears highlighted in the chat. Viewers can also purchase Super Stickers, which is a digital or animated image that pops up in the live chat feed. Channels with many subscribers can often earn quite a bit of money from viewers sending them these chats and stickers during live stream videos. For those with huge channels, a Super Chat is often the only way for a viewer to be noticed by a creator during a live stream, as the creator will hear a notification sound when they receive a donation, and the comment or sticker is highlighted in the chat stream.

PATREON: Patreon is a membership service that some YouTube creators utilize to earn additional income. Some channels use Patreon like a tip jar, while others have multiple membership levels, each with varying perks, such as exclusive videos and merchandise.

Patreon is a more profitable option than YouTube Memberships, as Patreon creators keep more of their profits. However, YouTube Memberships keep everything organized in your channel dashboard. It's really a preference of the creator which they choose.

TIP JAR: Just as some creators use Patreon as a virtual tip jar, you can also collect tips on your blog, website, or YouTube channel in several ways, including by providing your audience with your PayPal, Stripe, or Venmo email. A simple message such as "If you would like to support my channel with a virtual tip, you can send it to" with the email address associated with your account.

YOUTUBE FINANCIAL STATISTICS

- YouTube generates 11% of Google's total ad revenue
- YouTube partners have been paid out over 2 billion US dollars
- YouTube channels that earn more than $100,000 per year also grow more than 40% year over year
- YouTube pays an average of $4 for every 1000 video views
- The top earning YouTube channel is MrBeast at 54 million
- YouTube Premium has over 50 million subscribers
- YouTube's global advertising revenue was nearly 30 billion dollars in 2021

CHAPTER SIX: YOUTUBE ACCOUNTING MADE EASY

As you start this chapter, I know what you might be thinking: "I want to start a YouTube channel, not worry about accounting!"

Well, that is the catch when it comes to making money online: Like it or not, you must pay taxes on the money you earn, and that includes what you earn on YouTube! While it would be great to keep all the AdSense money you earn every month, if you earn more than $600 in a year from your channel, you will be giving a cut to Uncle Sam every year.

And whether you want to track your income or not, in the end, the IRS will come for their share of the money!

The good news is that YouTube bookkeeping is relatively easy! Unlike my Ebay and Etsy businesses, where I have considerable expenses and forms to keep track of, it is much easier to manage my YouTube income and expenses. However, it is still important that I do as there are tax write-offs associated with running my YouTube channel. Since Google AdSense issues YouTube Creators 1099 tax forms, we can also declare expenses as write-offs to pay less in taxes.

Before I dive deeper into how I manage my YouTube bookkeeping, please note that I am not an accountant. I PAY an accountant to file my taxes for me. But I do keep track of my income and expenses throughout the year. Be sure to consult with an accountant or tax professional in your area regarding your own personal tax obligations. The following advice is just that: Advice.

But even with an accountant handling my tax filing, I still need to provide him with my actual numbers. As I mentioned, I track my income and expenses throughout the year so that come tax time, I have my numbers ready to hand over to my accountant. My entire bookkeeping system can be found in my **2023 YouTube Channel Planner & Accounting Ledger: All-In-One Business & Bookkeeping Organizer for Online Content Creators & Influencers,** which is available exclusively on Amazon.

In addition to calendar and goal-setting pages, my planner also comes with accounting ledgers. The accounting ledgers provided in the planner are broken down into two sections: Income and Expenses. Income is the money you earn from YouTube, and expenses are the money you spend on your channel. There are monthly ledgers and year-end ones to make the entire process easy.

For example, every month, I record the following streams of income from my YouTube channel:

- **AdSense:** Money paid directly to YouTube creators from Google from the ads placed on videos. If you earn more than $600 in AdSense in a calendar year, Google will issue you a 1099 form.
- **Sponsorships:** Any money that a company pays you

to promote their products/services on your channel. Most companies do not provide 1099 forms, so you will manually need to track this money.
- **Affiliates:** Any money I earn from viewers buying something on Amazon through my Amazon Associates link, along with other money I earn from affiliate networks.

But the planner has room to record any possible income a YouTube creator might have. While these days I only have AdSense, Sponsorships, and Affiliates, as I mentioned, many creators have multiple income streams for their channels, including Memberships, Patreon, Merchandise, and even Donations.

Every year, Google sends me a 1099 form for the AdSense I earned from the ads on my channel. If you earn more than $600 in a year, Google will issue you a 1099 form. You can choose to have them mail the 1099 form to you, or you can print it off online. Do not worry: YouTube will notify you if and when your 1099 form is ready.

But even if you do not meet the $600 threshold to receive a 1099 form, you may still need to claim what you did earn on your taxes. Be sure to consult with an accountant or tax professional in your area, as some states have different rules than others. Any money you earn on YouTube, whether through AdSense, Memberships, or SuperChats, will be reflected on the 1099 form as it all comes from Google.

As for sponsorships, it depends on the company if they send you a 1099 form. Many do not, but you still need to track that income. I have personally never received a 1099 form from a sponsor, but I have also never made a large amount of money from sponsorships. You will need to ask any company that sponsors you what their policy is. Be sure to note how you will be paid and if they will be issuing you a tax form before you sign a contract.

Patreon sends users 1099 forms if they earn $20,000 in a year. However, if you live in Illinois, they will issue you a 1099 form if you earn $1000 or more in a year. If you live in Maryland, Massachusetts, Vermont, or Virginia, the threshold to receive a 1099 form is $600 or more in a year. But like sponsorships, even if you do not receive a tax form, you will likely still need to claim any money you earn from Patreon. Again, check with a professional in your area, as the laws vary by state.

Some YouTube creators set up donation links, and while it may not amount to very much, you still need to account for it. And if you are selling merchandise through TeeSpring or any other website, you'll need to track that, too. I sell merchandise through TeePublic, but they do not issue 1099 forms. However, I still have to track that income.

After you have tallied your gross income total related to your YouTube channel, you next need to make a note of your expenses. Since Google pays YouTube creators advertising royalties, YouTube is looked at as a business by the government. While this means you need to claim the money you make, it also means you can claim expenses as tax write-offs.

In my planner, I have space for you to record the following expenses:

Bank Fees: It is wise to set up a separate bank account for any business you have, including YouTube. Most banks charge checking account fees, but credit unions typically do not. If you already have a bank account, it is okay to stick with that for now. But if you start earning a large amount of money on YouTube, you will definitely want to consider a dedicated account just for your channel earnings.

Phone/Internet: Your smartphone and internet connection is essential for running your channel, meaning you can claim these as expenses. From the phone itself to the plan you are on, along with the internet connection you pay for, all are deductions you can claim on your taxes.

Equipment: Even the most basic YouTube setup (um, that would be mine, ha-ha!) requires equipment. Cameras, tripods, lighting, computers, and printers are all business expenses you can claim as business deductions.

Software/Subscriptions: Paying for editing software and graphic subscriptions can add up. Fortunately, these are business deductions for YouTubers. Do not forget any apps you pay for, as you can claim those, too.

Office Supplies: Copy paper, pens, and toner ink for your printer - these are all items you are likely using to manage your YouTube channel, so keep track of what you are spending on them.

Postage: If you do giveaways on your channel, you will likely pay money to ship out prizes. Keep track of how much you spend on postage and any shipping materials (boxes, envelopes, packing materials). Note that printing a shipping label online at usps.com costs less than taking packages to the Post Office. You can also arrange for FREE USPS Carrier Pickup of packages. I submit a request the night before for packages to be picked up when my mail carrier comes at his regular time.

Advertising: I occasionally run Facebook ads for my YouTube channel. Since I have a Facebook page, setting up advertisements on the site is easy. I also include business cards and any other promotional materials I buy in the "advertising" category.

Props: If you are spending money on your video backgrounds or buying things to show on camera, these items count as props, and you can claim them come tax time.

Giveaways: Giveaways can be a great way to grow your channel (I will discuss this more in the next chapter), so keep track of any money you spend on prizes.

Travel: If you travel at all for your channel, you can claim those expenses. I once claimed a Disney World vacation because I was researching a book!

Meals: You can claim any money you spend on meals if you are doing so for your channel. For instance, maybe you are treating a fellow creator with whom you are collaborating out to lunch. Or perhaps you are reviewing a restaurant for your channel. Keep those receipts and write down how much you spend.

Taxes: As your channel grows, you may find that you are making enough money that you will need to pay quarterly income tax. Quarterly income tax is something many small businesses schedule to avoid paying one large lump sum at the end of the year. I pay both state and federal quarterly taxes four times a year. An accountant can set this up for you.

My accountant prepares the forms I need to mail in; all I have to do is write the checks and address the envelopes. This does not mean that I will not still owe taxes, but it helps with a big chunk of it. If I earn more than anticipated, I will then still owe come tax time. But if my income was down, I may end up with a refund. Taxes are unavoidable, so again, consult with an accountant!

Mileage: You may not think you are driving much for your YouTube channel, but you likely are. If you are a vlogger, you definitely are. But even if you only film sit-down videos at home, you are likely still driving a bit in relation to your channel. Whether it is going to the Post Office or buying giveaway prizes at a local store, be sure to track your mileage as you can deduct it come tax time. You can download several free apps to your smartphone to track your mileage. My favorite is MileIQ which tracks your miles just by the movement of your phone while in the car.

At the end of every month, add up your gross income numbers and then add up your expenses. Subtract your expenses from your total gross income to get your monthly NET PROFIT. Then at the end of the year, tally up each individual category to get your year-end numbers. These total numbers of income and expenses are what your accountant will need to prepare your taxes.

Having to hand over a chuck of your hard-earned money to the government is not fun for anyone, but it is a fact of life. And if you want to be successful on YouTube and make money on the site, you will have to deal with taxes. Find a good local accountant who understands small home-based businesses with 1099 forms to file. The expense of a good accountant is worth it to have your taxes filed correctly!

HIGHEST PAID YOUTUBE CREATORS:

1. MrBeast $54 million
2. Jake Paul $45 million
3. Markiplier $38 million
4. Rhett & Link $30 million
5. Unspeakable $28.5 million
6. Nastya $28 million
7. Ryan Kaji $27 million
8. Dude Perfect $20 million
9. Logan Paul $18 million
10. Preston Arsement $16 million

CHAPTER SEVEN: MARKETING & PROMOTION

If you really want to establish a presence on YouTube and earn money from your videos, you will have to do everything you can to promote your channel and build your brand. YouTube is a social media platform, and you want to use all the other social media sites available to you to draw traffic to your videos. More traffic equals more views, which in turn equals more AdSense revenue, which can also lead to sponsorship opportunities as your channel grows.

Fortunately, the social media sites that will bring you the most traffic are all free and easy to use. And it is likely that you already have accounts on some or even all of them. And once you get into the habit of promoting your videos via social media, it becomes second nature and is a quick step to complete every time you upload a new video.

Setting up your various social networking sites is yet another reason why it is so essential that you choose the best YouTube channel name possible right out of the gate. You want to be known under the same name everywhere to establish your brand.

I am now "Ann Eckhart" on my main YouTube channel as well as on Facebook, Twitter, Instagram, TikTok, and Pinterest. I use the same photo across all my sites, too, so that no matter what website someone is browsing, when they see "Ann Eckhart" and my picture, they know it is me.

My second channel may be called "Ann Eckhart Vlogs," but I still promote it under my "Ann Eckhart" brand as it is easier to have one social media account identity across various sites. I use different photos and channel graphics to differentiate my vlog channel from my main channel.

However, both of my channels and their accompanying social media sites used to have different names: SeeAnnSave and SeeAnnAtWDW, respectively. Renaming everything was a huge hassle. And while it made sense for me to do since my content changed drastically, hopefully, you will be sticking with one "brand" for your YouTube journey. Trust me that it's easier to build from one place than try to backtrack from multiple places the way I did.

While I do YouTube for fun, it is also a business for me. Everything I create regarding my channel is done to promote it as a brand. My videos drive traffic to my books, and my books drive traffic to my channel. My social media sites promote both my books and my YouTube channel. And they all drive traffic to my Ebay store and Etsy shop. It is a trifecta of promotion: YouTube, books, and social media all work together to drive traffic to each other, which grows my audience and results in more book sales, more affiliate income, and more AdSense dollars. And it also brings in more customers to my Ebay and Etsy listings.

Whenever I get burned out on YouTube or discouraged because my channel isn't as growing as fast as others, I remind myself that YouTube is just one piece of my entire business portfolio. Even if I didn't earn money from YouTube, I would still make videos as they are essentially free advertising for my other business ventures.

This chapter will cover all of the possible ways you can market your videos to grow your channel. Note that you do not have to do any of these if you do not want to, and you certainly do not have to do all of them. However, some social media promotion is beneficial in promoting your videos. So even if you are not currently using social media, give it a chance to grow your channel.

BLOG/WEBSITE: Most successful YouTube creators have coordinating blogs or websites, some even starting those sites before creating YouTube channels. What is great about a blog or a website is they are additional ways to earn AdSense dollars. When you have both a blog and a monetized YouTube channel, you have two AdSense income sources.

Plus, you can place other ads on your site through affiliate and referral programs and directly from selling advertising to companies. Many affiliate programs, including Amazon, even provide you with banner ads that you can place on your website.

Before starting my last blog, I had dabbled in blogging a few times on Blogger, which is Google's blog platform. I originally had a blog dedicated solely to my Ebay business. However, when I started *AnnEckhart.com*, I closed the former blog and moved all content to the new website.

Note that I am speaking in the past tense as in 2021 when I chose to close my blog down. Since I was only using it as a place to post my new YouTube videos, I honestly did not see it serving a purpose anymore. It had become expensive, and I was constantly having site issues; shutting it down worked best for me.

However, I still want to talk to you about having a blog, as it can benefit your channel. If YouTube were my primary income, I would likely have kept my blog. But even though I no longer have it, I will explain how the site worked for me when I had it so that you can see how it could work for you, too.

The difference between my first Ebay blog and my recent *AnnEckhart.com* blog was that my Ebay blog was just a blog, whereas my *AnnEckhart.com* blog was technically a website that hosted my blog. In essence, it was a blog ON a website.

Confused? Do not worry; I was, and still am sometimes, when trying to explain the difference! Even today, I struggle with whether to call my former site a blog or a website. In the beginning, I called it a website, but toward the end, I called it a blog, even though it was technically a website, mainly because the term "blog" is more prevalent in the social media world. Oy!

Simply put, a blog on a free platform such as Blogger or WordPress is just a blog. However, a website is an actual site that you own that utilizes blogging software. *AnnEckhart.com* was my website, and on my website, I used WordPress blogging software.

Oh, and on a side note: I still own the *AnnEckhart.com* URL! I just now have it pointed to my Amazon Storefront. There I have all of my books, business supplies, and household favorites linked for my viewers to find. I earn royalties from my book sales and affiliate income from the sale of supplies and recommended products. So, I earn commissions on top of commissions!

But back to the topic at hand:

When you have a blog on a free site, it is not yours but instead belongs to the company behind the site you are using, which means that it could be shut down at any time, resulting in you losing all your content. And while Blogger and WordPress have been around for years and show no signs of going anywhere, the risk is still there that you could eventually lose all your content.

I had my blog set up through Bluehost (bluehost.com), and I used WordPress software. This was a different setup than just starting a free blog on a site such as Blogger or WordPress. Since

I was using a hosting company, I actually OWNED my website. I paid Bluehost for all their hosting services and features, one of which was the WordPress blogging software. I decided to go the route of paying for my site so that it could not be taken down. If Blogger or WordPress were to suddenly shut down (not likely to happen, of course, but you never know), I would still have had my website as I own it through a hosting company.

Having an actual website that incorporates a blogging platform also allowed me many more options for customization. I could do much more with my Bluehost site than I could if I were going directly through WordPress, for example. Bluehost offers numerous free plug-ins for their sites, including those for placing AdSense ads. I simply installed one of the free AdSense plug-ins, clicked where I wanted ads to show, and the ads were automatically placed. I then earned AdSense money from those ads. And I could change the ad placements and sizes at any time.

I looked at my website as my "homepage" for everything I did. I could share my videos there as well as my books. I could post updates, which automatically went out to anyone who subscribed to receive them. I had my affiliate and referral links organized along with links to all of my social media pages. I even had an entire section devoted to my recipes, which were very popular with my followers.

When I spoke with someone who asked about my YouTube channel or books, it was much easier for me to direct them to *AnnEckhart.com* than it was trying to explain how they could find my YouTube channel or my books on Amazon. *AnnEckhart.com* was the leading portal for my "brand."

Today, as I mentioned, the *AnnEckhart.com* URL points to my Amazon Author Page. Since my books are currently my primary income, that is where I want people to go. If I was doing YouTube full-time, I could easily point the URL to my channel. When you purchase URLs through sites such as GoDaddy.com, you have the ability to point your URLs to any site you like. And it is easy to change, too. When I decided not to renew my blog, I went into my GoDaddy account and pointed my URLs away from the blog and over to my books.

So, do I miss having a blog, especially for sharing my YouTube videos? While having a coordinating blog or website can be helpful, note that it is not a requirement. Many successful YouTube creators do not have any sort of website. While they may utilize some additional social media sites to promote themselves, many focus solely on their channel. In fact, there are quite a number of successful YouTube creators who ONLY utilize YouTube and barely, if at all, post on any other social media platforms.

Focusing solely on your channel certainly makes the most sense when you are just starting out on YouTube. After you have been on YouTube for a while, if you feel like you really want to grow your channel, you can start branching out to other social media platforms. You will want to explore all of the free social media sites before deciding if you want to invest money into your website.

When I had my Ebay blog on Blogger, I did not put anything significant on it; I just posted about new listings in my store and had the links to my social networking sites. I rarely even promoted the blog; I just maintained it so that if anyone happened to stumble across it, they would hopefully click through to my Ebay store.

However, my *AnnEckhart.com* blog was a business for me as I earned income through affiliate advertising and referral links, not to mention that it drove traffic to my YouTube channel and to my books. If my site had been on a free blogging platform, all of my information could have been lost at a moment's notice. However, as long as I kept paying my website maintenance fees, my content was safe and belonged to me.

Oh, the cost? Yup, having a website costs money! I spent several hundred dollars every year maintaining my hosting contract, as well as plug-ins and URLs. I no longer feel the cost is worth it for me, but again, it may end up being different for you.

I've mentioned a few times now that I have an Etsy shop. I sell stickers and magnets in my shop, which is called Jean Lee Publishing. In addition to writing books like the one you are reading under my legal name, I also sell journals, planners, notebooks, and adult coloring books under the Jean Lee pen name.

In 2022, I started a website through GoDaddy at jeanleepublishing.com. In addition to URLs, you can also pay for a website through GoDaddy. I decided to start a small site where I could promote my "Jean Lee" brand in one place. If you go to the site, you'll see I have links to my Etsy sticker shop and other links to my journals, planners, notebooks, and coloring books. Because I essentially have two different sites that I am selling on – Etsy and Amazon – and since I sell a wide variety of different products between the two, having a dedicated website for my brand made sense.

But for my main brand, which is AnnEckhart.com, the most important place I want to direct people is my Amazon Storefront. My books are my primary source of income. Not YouTube, not Ebay, not Etsy. If I can only choose one place to send people, I want it to by Amazon. I don't want to confuse people by having my main site jumbled in with all my other sites.

And that is what you will need to decide for yourself in terms of starting a blog or website. What is the most important place you want to send people to? If it's YouTube, then you are fine with just pointing people there.

If you do decide to pursue having your own website, I personally would not even bother creating a blog on a free platform as you do not want to spend time driving traffic to a site that you might eventually want to change. If you are absolutely sure that you want to start your own site, I would go straight to a paid version so that you own it right out of the gate. A website is something that can wait until you are further along in your YouTube career.

If you decide to go with a paid website, do your research, as there are many companies out there to choose from. I went with a large company (bluehost.com) because I wanted my blog to be the centerpiece of my brand and to utilize several forms of affiliate advertising.

However, there are a lot of low-cost website options out there. For instance, you can not only register for website URLs on GoDaddy (godaddy.com), but they also offer website hosting along with easy-to-create websites and blogs. I personally use a GoDaddy website that is attached to a fiction pen name I use. It is a basic site but comes with my URL cost and does the basic job I need it to do.

So, which should you choose? A free blog or a website? Or no site at all? That is a decision only you can make. Having a blog or website for your YouTube channel is NOT a requirement. In fact, it may be more work than is worth it for you. And as I talk about in the next section, you may find that a Facebook page can just as easily act as your "website."

However, it does not have to be complicated if you decide to set up a blog or website. Think of it as your brand's "home" page to provide the links to your videos and all your social networking sites. I mentioned my jeanleepublishing.com website, which is a very simple, inexpensive site that I have through GoDaddy. My only purpose with the site is to steer people in the right direction of either my Etsy shop or Amazon print-on-demand products. I don't need to clutter up the site with links to my YouTube channel.

One significant benefit of having a blog is that you can run giveaways there. YouTube no longer allows you to host giveaways on your channel or videos. You are not allowed to tie in giveaway requirements to your videos, meaning you cannot instruct people to enter a giveaway by subscribing to your channel, giving a video a "thumbs up," or leaving a comment. You can announce giveaways in your videos, but you must direct people somewhere else to enter.

Hence, a website comes in handy for hosting giveaways, as people can enter directly on your site. When I did giveaways, I first wrote up a post detailing the prize and entrance requirements and directed people to enter by leaving comments on the post. I then randomly drew the winner or winners from the entries. Or I sometimes used a site such as Random.org to insert a code that allowed people to enter the giveaway quickly and made it easy for me to draw the winner. Because people had to submit their email addresses to enter the giveaways, I just emailed the winner to obtain their mailing address to send them their prize.

It is important to note that Facebook has the same policy as YouTube regarding giveaways because you cannot run them on their site on a public page. You can, however, run them if you have a private Facebook group, which I will discuss in the next section. Just note that if you plan to do giveaways, you will need to have a site other than YouTube or Facebook to host them. You can, however, run the giveaways on Twitter or Instagram. I favor Instagram as it is easy to contact the winners via Instagram's messaging system.

Note that in addition to posting updates on your blog, you will also need to maintain it. If you allow visitors to leave comments on your posts, you will want to make sure to respond to them. You also want to maintain all links to ensure they are active and up to date so that people do not click through and get an error.

You will also want to secure a URL or several URLs for your website. I use GoDaddy.com to purchase my URLs; I own not only *AnnEckhart.com* but also several iterations of my name and my Ebay store, Etsy shop, and other businesses I own. While .com is the most popular suffix, there are many other options you might want to consider owning as well, such as .org, .info, .net, etc. Each of these additional options comes with an added price.

It is an added expense to purchase URL addresses, but if you are serious about building a brand, it is an investment you will want to make. You can purchase URLs for a minimum of one year, although you will likely save some money if you commit to a longer-term.

Here are the top sites to purchase URLs, also called "domain names," from:

Bluehost: I have talked about how I used Bluehost to host my blog, but you can also register URLs through them. They are the official WordPress hosting partner; WordPress was the software I used to run my blog. Learn more at bluehost.com.

Domain.com: In addition to purchasing URLs, Domain.com also offers a Website Builder and email account. Learn more at Domain.com.

GoDaddy: Probably the most recognizable name in the domain business, GoDaddy manages over 77 million URLs for over 18 million customers. As I have mentioned, it is the site I use for purchasing my domains, and I also utilize their website and email services. Learn more at godaddy.com.

HostGator: HostGator offers domain and website hosting and is an ideal site for beginners. Learn more at hostgator.com.

Network Solutions: In addition to domain registration, Network Solutions offers web hosting, a website builder, security tools, email addresses, marketing, SEO services, and IT support. Learn more at NetworkSolutions.com.

FACEBOOK: If you want to "brand" yourself and your YouTube channel, you will want to set up a Facebook page. Facebook offers more ways to connect with your audience than Twitter, Pinterest, and Instagram combined. And if you do not want the hassle of maintaining a blog or separate site, a Facebook page can efficiently act as your dedicated "website."

YouTube makes it easy to share your videos on Facebook as a "share" button is located under all videos. Simply click on the Facebook icon, link your YouTube and Facebook accounts together, and you can then share your YouTube videos on your personal and/or business page.

Note that while you may have a personal Facebook account, you will want to set up a Facebook PAGE for your YouTube channel. A Facebook business page differs from a personal Facebook page, although you first need to have a personal account and page to set up a business page.

A business page is one people "like," while a personal page is one where people "friend" you. A personal Facebook page limits the number of "friends" you can have, but you can have limitless "likes" on your business page. Plus, having a business page also allows you to separate your personal and public life.

My personal Facebook page is private and is only for my personal friends and family to see. However, my "Ann Eckhart" Facebook page is public; anyone can view it and "like" it to be notified when I post there. Since my public page is a business page, it also allows me to accept sponsorships from companies that pay me to post about their products on my feed.

As your YouTube channel grows, you will likely find that viewers want to "friend" you on your personal Facebook page. Even if you are not promoting your personal page, it will still be easy for most people to find. Unless it is a subscriber you have gotten to know very well, I strongly encourage you NOT to add subscribers as friends on Facebook. You want to maintain privacy with a division between your personal and public/business life.

While many of my friends and family "like" my Facebook business page, not all do. Keeping my personal page private protects me and my friends and family from exposing their information to my business page followers. You can try to "hide" your personal Facebook page by not using your photo in your profile picture and by using a different name, such as your first and middle name or a maiden name if you have one.

I use my Facebook business page to promote my YouTube videos and books and save my personal information for my personal Facebook account. While it is hard to turn down friend requests from well-meaning people, I only accept Facebook "friend" requests from my actual friends and family for safety and security reasons. YouTube subscribers and readers of my books need to "like" my Facebook business page to connect with me.

I have set up my personal Facebook page with the tightest security settings to protect myself. I have also turned off the private messaging settings on my business page so people cannot send me messages. When I allowed people to message me, I found myself inundated with long notes from people wanting advice on Ebay, help with publishing, or just someone to chat with. While most of these messages were harmless, it took a lot of my time and energy to deal with all the questions.

Again, just as it is hard to deny friend requests, it can be hard to ignore messages from well-meaning followers. However, I always remind myself that I am not just running my businesses, including my YouTube channel, for profit. In other words, I need the money to pay my bills! And while YouTube has never been my primary source of income, I am continuously growing my brand for the long term. Therefore, I treat everything I do as a business. I also must protect myself and my family by guarding my personal information as much as possible. Hence why I am so protective of my online privacy.

A Facebook page needs "likes" to grow. While it can take a while to build up the number of "likes" on a business page, I still believe setting one up separately from your personal account is essential. I have seen many people start out using their personal Facebook account for their online content, only to reach the maximum number of "friends" allowed eventually. They then had to scramble to create a business page and encourage everyone to "like" it. Facebook users are more accustomed to "friending" people than "liking" pages, so it does take longer to build a business page than a friend list.

To set up a Facebook business page, simply visit **facebook.com/about/pages.**

You will need to log into your personal Facebook account first, and then the system will walk you through the steps necessary to create your business page. Creating a Facebook business page is free and easy to do, and I consider it an essential step in establishing your brand and building your YouTube channel.

The first decision you will need to make is to **name your business's Facebook page**. My Facebook business page is *Ann Eckhart*, the same name as my books and YouTube channel, not to mention the name I use on my other social media accounts. You will also want your page name to match your YouTube channel name.

As you create more social media accounts, you will want your name to be the same across all platforms. Remember, the goal is to BRAND yourself so that people will recognize you on all forms of social media. Therefore, now is the time to ensure you are happy with your channel name.

There are all kinds of things you can personalize on your Facebook page. You want to add a profile picture and a banner. I have a headshot as my profile picture, and I make my own customized banners for social media on apps like *Canva* and *WordSwag*.

Whatever photos or graphics you choose, remember that this is your BUSINESS page, so keep it professional. You do not want to post potentially controversial photographs of yourself; look at other YouTube creators' Facebook pages to get an idea of the kinds of photos and graphics that are acceptable to share.

You will also want to fill out the extensive **About** section of your page to provide people with information about your YouTube channel. However, since this is your BUSINESS page and separate from your personal page, you will want to be careful with how much information you share. While you may have your cell phone number available on your personal page to keep in touch with family and friends, unless you have a brick-and-mortar location that you want people to call, you will want to leave that section blank on your business page.

You will first need to choose the **Category** for your page; as a YouTube creator, there are several categories you can choose from, such as "Public Figure," "Entertainer," or "Personal Blog or Website." I prefer the latter; please do not dub yourself a public figure or celebrity until you reach at least a million subscribers. Touting yourself as something other than you will turn off potential followers. "Entertainer" or "Entertainment" is less offensive than "Public Figure," in my opinion.

You will need to select a sub-category for your Facebook page, too. And do not worry about being locked into your selections; you can easily change them anytime. In fact, Facebook regularly updates the options, so it is always good to check them a couple of times a year to see if better selections have been added.

In addition to your **Name** (the name of your page, i.e., your YouTube channel name), you can edit your Facebook URL so that it ends in that name. This provides you with a clickable URL link that you will want to provide on both your YouTube channel's "About" section and in the description box under all of your videos. The URL for my Facebook page is facebook.com/anneckhart.

Once you have created your Facebook business page, you can fill in the **About** section. You can enter your location here, although I keep this field blank to protect my privacy. Next up are **two description fields,** one short and one long. I have one simple sentence in the first field (Ann Eckhart is an author, YouTube content creator, and Ebay seller based in Iowa.). I provide a bit more information in the second field (*Welcome to the official Facebook page of Ann Eckhart (formerly SeeAnnSave)! I am an author, vlogger, influencer, and Ebayer. I am also a pug dog mom, caregiver, and Walt Disney World fanatic!*). Again, you can edit these fields anytime, so do not worry about being locked into what you first type in.

Next, you will see **your page's statistics**, including how many people "like" your page and how many people "follow" the page. Underneath these numbers will be a **field to enter one website URL**. If you create your Facebook page specifically to promote your YouTube channel, you will want to put your channel URL into this field. I have my Amazon Author Page linked here, but regardless; you will be able to further link your other sites down on the page.

In the next section, you can enter a **phone number**; however, you should leave this field blank unless you want strangers to call you. There are also fields for you to post your **email address** (I have a business email that I share across all of my accounts; I just use the one that I set up in Google when I started my YouTube channel), **additional categories** (these are Facebook's versions of "tags"; I chose "writer," "author," and "video creator"); and finally, there is space to post **all of your other links** (I have links to my Instagram, Twitter, and Pinterest pages as well as both of my YouTube channels here).

You will also want to take some time to customize your page's **Settings**, the link for which can be found on the left side of your page. There are lots of options available for you to edit here; I am going to share with you what mine are and why I chose them

- **Page Visibility:** Page published (obviously, as my page is public on Facebook!)
- **Visitor Posts:** Disable posts by other people on the page (I chose this setting to prevent anyone from sharing their posts on my page; this is mainly done to control

spam and trolls.)
- **Post and Story Sharing:** Allow Sharing To Stories (This allows my followers to share my posts with their Facebook friends, which can help me gain more followers and/or clicks through to my Amazon Author Page and YouTube channels.)
- **Audience Optimization for Posts** (I personally left this blank)
- **Messages:** I do not allow people to contact my Page privately by showing them the Messaging buttons. This is a personal decision; if you feel comfortable having your followers message you through Facebook, then you can select this option.
- **Tagging Ability:** I do not allow others to tag photos and videos published by my page to maintain control over my content.
- **Others Tagging This Page:** I do not allow these options for the same reason of maintaining control over my content.
- **Country Restriction:** I have none selected.
- **Age Restrictions:** I chose Public, but there are also options for ages 17 and up, 18 and up, 19 and up, 21 and up, and Alcohol-Related.
- **Page Moderation:** I left this field blank, but you can block posts or comments that contain specific words.
- **Profanity Filter:** I have this turned Off, but you can also select from Medium or Strong.
- **Similar Page Suggestions:** I selected for my page to be included when recommending similar Facebook Pages that people might like on a Page timeline.
- **Page Updates:** I automatically select to publish posts when info is uploaded on my page.
- **Post in Multiple Languages:** I have this turned off as I only know English!
- **Translate Automatically:** However, I have selected Facebook to show people who understand other

- languages automatic translations of my posts when available.
- **Comment Ranking:** I chose for Facebook to show me the most relevant comments by default.
- **Content Distribution:** I have not chosen to prohibit downloading to Facebook.

Finally, there are options to **Download Page** and **Merge Page**, providing you with links to complete those tasks if you so desire (I have never used these). And the last option is to **Remove Page**, which will delete your page so that nobody will see it or find it. If you ever select to delete your page, you will have 14 days to restore it if you change your mind.

Once you have your Facebook business page set up, it is time to start building your audience by getting people to "Like" your page. You will be able to invite friends and family on your personal page to "Like" your new business page. And, of course, you can promote your Facebook page on your YouTube channel by adding your page URL to the "About" section on YouTube and providing the link under all of your videos.

After all of your Facebook and other social media accounts are active, you will want to make sure to provide links to all your pages in the "About" information section of your YouTube channel home page, plus in the description box under each video. Note that you need to enter the full URL address of your sites, including the "http://" as only the complete "http" links will be active, allowing viewers to click through to the sites directly.

To make this process easy, I have my full description bar write-up and links in a Word document that I simply copy and paste into the description box of every video I upload. I will discuss this further in *Chapter Nine: A Day in the Life*.

As I mentioned earlier, I ensure all my social networking accounts and websites work together to drive as much traffic as possible to my videos. When I upload a new YouTube video, I post the link to Facebook. Unfortunately, Facebook has made it increasingly difficult for people to see posts, hiding posts from business pages as they want those of us with pages to pay for the posts to be seen. This is frustrating, but there are some things you can do to help your posts be seen.

Once you have a business page and start posting there, you will likely notice the **Boost** buttons under posts that encourage you to pay for your updates to be directly shown to your followers. And while it can be tempting to spend $5 or more to ensure your posts are seen, resist the urge to boost everything you put on Facebook, as the results are not worth the cost. Instead, perhaps spend $5 every other week or so to promote one post to see if it affects your page "likes" and/or your YouTube subscriber growth.

I personally choose one video per week to "boost" on Facebook, typically one that is already performing well. You might be wondering why I would focus on a video that is already getting views. The reason is "low-hanging fruit." It is better to promote your best-selling products, in this case, a video that is performing well, in the hopes that it will bring people to your other products, in this case, the other videos on your channel.

I utilize this technique when I run ads for my books. I only advertise my best sellers. These books sell well without advertising, but my books' sales increase when I advertise them. Why? Because if someone buys one of my books and enjoys it, they are likely to come back and purchase another of my titles. And since my best sellers are my best reviewed, I want to start them off with my best books.

The same is true for running ads on a well-performing YouTube video. If many people are organically finding and watching a particular video, it only makes sense that others will join in once they see it is popular.

Think about it like this: Say you saw an ad for a product with no reviews. Amazon products will show the number of stars a product has received, which indicates how popular an item is. You may get an ad for a product with no reviews, but then you get an ad for a product with thousands of reviews. When choosing between the two, most people will choose the product with the most reviews.

In the same way, on YouTube, viewers go with the videos with the most views. Let's say you do a search for "best vlogging camera" on YouTube. The results show you various videos that all look relatively the same. The only difference is the number of views they have. If you must choose one, will you watch the video with only a few dozen views or the video with thousands of views? I am betting that you choose the one that the most people have watched.

If you have a video that is performing well on YouTube, that is the one I would choose to "boost" on Facebook. Boosting a post turns your post into an ad that will be shown to the audience you specify. Facebook can target your ad to who they think will be the most interested in it, or you can narrow down your audience.

When I boost a post that features a YouTube video, I choose for Facebook to target the people who "like" my page AND the people who are connected to them (the friends and family of the people who already "like" my page). You have likely seen ads in your Facebook feed and have noticed that the ad shows you which of your Facebook friends like that company. Seeing that your friends already like a company will make you more likely to click on the ad.

However, if you are new in your YouTube journey, you likely have very few people who "like" your page. In this case, I would recommend that you let Facebook choose the audience they will show the ad to. You can set a low budget – like I said, even just $5 – for a few days and see how it performs.

Because Facebook is selective about what posts they will show your followers, it is essential to do more than just post links to your Facebook page to engage your audience. Facebook prefers original posts and photos over links that you simply copy and paste to your page.

I try to post a regular status update at least once a day, which is more likely to be shown to my followers than a post with a link that I share directly from my blog. I also occasionally share photos on my Facebook page; like status updates, pictures tend to show up to more people than just links to my blog. Since my Facebook and Instagram accounts are linked, it is easy to share whatever I post to Instagram to Facebook. That way, I can knock out two social media posts in just one step.

Another way to engage your Facebook page users is to post "teasers" for upcoming videos. Post a photo of yourself as you are prepping to film or a picture of something you are getting ready to share, with the message that a new video will be coming the next day. This will get people excited about your latest video being released.

You want to encourage people to "like" and "comment" on your Facebook posts in the hopes their activity will show up on their friends' feeds, which will help more people come to your page. As I mentioned, for Facebook ads, you have likely seen this happen on your Facebook feed, where it will show you that a friend liked a post or a page. The convenient "like" thumbs-up icon will be there, making it easy for you to "like" the page.

I hope that when someone "likes" one of my posts, their friends will see it, check out my page, and then "like" it, too. As I mentioned earlier, Facebook shows status updates and photos more than links; so, I get more "likes" and comments on my status updates and pictures than I do when I simply share links to my blog posts or videos.

Also, as I mentioned earlier, you may decide that a Facebook page can act like your blog or website rather than setting up a separate site. Many YouTube creators do not have a blog or website, preferring to use Facebook as their homepage. So, unless you have the time to maintain a separate website, consider just using Facebook and other social networking sites to promote your YouTube channel. I recommend you do Facebook FIRST, as you can always add a blog/website later in your journey.

Another Facebook option is to form a private group. Again, this is something you will want to consider when you have more followers. But a private group where you can interact with your viewers is a popular way to engage your audience.

As I discussed earlier in the book, I used to have a blog called SeeAnnSave, where I shared free samples, coupons, and clearance deals. I also used to put a lot of that type of money-saving content on YouTube. When I closed my blog, I heard from many readers who missed it. So, I created a private Facebook group where I now post the deals I used to share on my blog.

You can do the same with your YouTube videos, posting videos in a private group before they go live, answering viewer questions, and holding giveaways. Anything you can do to create "brand" loyalty is always a good idea, and Facebook makes that easy and free!

TWITTER: If you do not already have a Twitter account, you can create one at **Twitter.com.** If you do have an account that you are active on, consider creating a new one just for your YouTube channel.

As with Facebook, you want to keep your personal and business lives separate on Twitter. Make sure your Twitter handle is the same as your YouTube channel. Remember, part of branding is being known as ONE name across ALL social media platforms. You will need a different email address for each Twitter account you create; since you were given a Gmail address when you signed up for a Google account and YouTube channel, you can use that one.

Like Facebook, Twitter provides a free and easy way to connect with viewers and drive traffic to your YouTube videos. YouTube makes sharing your videos to Twitter super easy as there is a Twitter share button under all videos. Simply click on the Twitter icon and link your YouTube account to your Twitter account to share the title of your video and the direct link and thumbnail of your video.

Twitter allows users to share posts of 280 characters or less. While your video's title, the link, and the thumbnail will automatically be put into the Twitter field, you can increase your exposure by adding hashtags. **Hashtags** are simply keywords that follow a pound (#) sign. For instance, when I film a video about selling on Ebay, I will use hashtags such as:

- #ebay
- #ebayseller
- #reselling
- #makingmoneyonline
- #homebasedbusiness
- #youtube
- #video

I try to add as many hashtags as I have room for as savvy Twitter users search for tweets using hashtags, which increases the chance of you driving traffic to your videos.

When you share a YouTube video to Twitter, Twitter automatically tags the official YouTube Twitter account in your tweet. Please do not remove the tag as it is another free and easy way to get more views as people who follow YouTube potentially might see the tag and click to watch your video.

I set aside some time every evening to connect with other Twitter users since I can do this on my iPhone while relaxing in front of the TV. I follow other resellers and YouTube creators, retweet posts I like, reply to posts and post a Tweet or two of my own. Twitter works best when you actively engage with other users, so spending some time each day networking on Twitter to grow your followers is crucial.

Some Twitter users follow everyone who follows them, which can certainly be a way to build up your followers. You can also "network" with other folks on Twitter by replying to, retweeting, or favoring tweets. As I mentioned, when setting up your Facebook page, you can add all your social media links, including your Twitter URL, in the "About" section of your Facebook business page; hopefully, some of your Facebook fans will follow you on Twitter. To encourage this, about once a week, post your Twitter link directly to your Facebook page to make it easy for people to click through and "follow" you.

Add your Twitter URL to the list of other links you share on your YouTube channel, both in your channel information section as well as under each video. Remember to add the http:// to your link to make it active so that users can directly click through to your Twitter account.

The **Edit Profile** feature located on your Twitter homepage allows you to customize the look and information people will see when they click on your profile. Add a nice, clear photo of yourself (or your logo, if you have one), and add a header image. Write up a brief but fun description of yourself. Put the link to your YouTube channel in the website field so people can click through to your videos. And finally, click on "theme colors" to customize your profile page even further.

Note that Twitter is decreasing in popularity as of late, so do not fret if you do not find yourself gaining a lot of followers. Nowadays, most people simply search for hashtags when using Twitter; they may find your post, but they are not as likely as they once were to follow you. However, the main goal is for people to click on and watch your videos. As long as your tweets are accomplishing that, do not worry if you are gaining followers or not.

Personalizing your Twitter profile, posting regularly, using hashtags, and engaging with other users daily will increase people finding your YouTube videos and subscribing to your channel, therefore earning you more AdSense revenue. And if you do end up growing a large Twitter following, you will be able to negotiate sponsored content in your feed.

PINTEREST: Pinterest is often overlooked when it comes to promoting YouTube videos, but, as with Facebook and Twitter, it is another free and easy way to drive traffic to your channel and increase your video views. And increased views mean more AdSense dollars!

If you do not already have a Pinterest account, you can create one at **pinterest.com**. If you are already an active Pinterest user, you can just do what I have done and add a "YouTube Videos" board to your account. However, if you have a very diverse Pinterest account with content that is irrelevant to your YouTube videos, you may consider setting up a second account. My content tends to be similar, so it is okay for me to have a "board" for my videos.

Pinterest allows you to create boards where you pin content. You can "pin" content that others have posted, and you can also share your own "pins." Pinterest started as a way for people, mainly women, to "pin" craft ideas and recipes to virtual boards. However, Pinterest is quickly becoming a tool for businesses to get the word out about their products and develop brand loyalty. And as you grow your YouTube brand, you will want to make Pinterest a part of your marketing strategy.

As I mentioned, I have a board on Pinterest that I titled *"YouTube Videos."* As with Facebook and Twitter, YouTube provides a "share" icon for Pinterest underneath all videos. After uploading a video to YouTube, I simply click on the Pinterest icon and "pin" it to my *"YouTube Videos"* board. The video then appears on the feed of those who follow me on Pinterest. They can click through to my video directly from my pin. And if they "repin" the post, then their followers will also see it. I noticed a dramatic increase in traffic to my books and my YouTube channel since I started pinning my links to my books and videos on Pinterest.

Just as you should be doing with your Facebook and Twitter

links, be sure to link your Pinterest page to your YouTube channel profile and the description bar underneath all your videos. And put the link in your Facebook page's "General Information" section. Be sure to periodically share your Pinterest link on both Facebook and Twitter to attract new followers.

You may be noticing by now that a big part of social networking is to have all your sites working together. Include all your social media links on your blog/website and Facebook. Post your Twitter and Pinterest links to Facebook. Share your Facebook and Pinterest links on Twitter. Ensure all your sites are drawing traffic to each other, which will help grow your brand and audience. The more you can get your YouTube channel link out there, the easier it will be for people to find your videos and for your channel to grow!

INSTAGRAM: Instagram offers another free, easy, and fun way to interact with your YouTube subscribers and gain more viewers. In fact, in just the past year or so, Instagram has brought my YouTube channel more traffic than Facebook, Twitter, and Pinterest combined.

To create an Instagram account, go to **Instagram.com.** Again, ensure your Instagram name is the same as your YouTube channel and other social media sites. If you already have a personal Instagram account, consider creating a second one specifically for your YouTube channel and brand.

Instagram allows you to share photos and "like" and comment on photos shared by others. While you cannot put a full-length YouTube video on Instagram, you can share content and put in links to your channel, both with your photos and in your profile.

And while you cannot add a full-length YouTube video to Instagram, you can add video there, both through **Stories** and through **Reels**, as well as one-minute-long **Posts**.

Instagram Stories: If you are already on Instagram, you likely know that small photos of the people you follow are at the top of the screen. When you click on a person's picture, you will see the "stories" they have posted, both photos and videos. This content remains on Instagram for 24 hours before it disappears. As long as there is a colorful ring around the photo, there is content to view.

Creating your own Instagram Story is simple. Just tap on the "+" icon at the top of the screen. Here you can choose to create a regular post, i.e., one that appears in your Instagram feed. Or you can choose **Story, Reels,** or **Live**. Choosing *Story* will allow you to upload a photo from your phone's camera roll or a short 15-second clip from your camera roll. Or you can create a photo or video clip right in the Instagram app by using the camera feature. This option is the large round white circle at the bottom of the page. In the same row are the various filters you can apply.

But let's focus on how to promote your YouTube channel in your stories. What I do is post the thumbnail of the video I want people to watch on my channel. I then add the direct link to the video so that viewers can simply tap it on the screen to go straight to my YouTube channel.

But what do you do if you have multiple links? What if you want to provide links to a website, social media accounts, and affiliate advertisers? It is easy, as you use an add-on feature called a "link tree," which allows you to create a page with multiple links that only requires one link in your profile to access.

Instagram only allows users to have ONE link in their profile. However, "link trees" enable multiple links. These link trees or landing pages are also used on TikTok, which also only allows one link in each bio.

Several companies provide link trees. Most have a basic free option with more advanced paid options. I recommend starting with a free option first, as you can always upgrade later if you feel you need to.

Some link tree/landing page options include:

Beacons: The only option that includes the ability to monetize links.

Campsite: Offers images next to the links for nice visual appeal.

ContactInBio: Considered a close second in popularity to Linktr.ee.

Link-in Profile: Instead of text links, you can add in your own images and make them clickable. The cost is $9.99 per month or $99 a year after a one-month free trial.

Linktr.ee: The first and arguably still the most popular of all the landing page sites. This is the one I use.

Lnk.bio: Minimalist design but limited features in the free version.

Milkshake: Unique in that it turns your "link in bio" into a free website.

Shorby: Features unlimited links and social icons but has no free option. Plans start at $9 per month.

TapBio: Pulls all data from Instagram and YouTube to create clickable "cards."

Once you have your link situation set up and are comfortable using Instagram Stories, it is time to take it up a notch and try Instagram's newest feature: "Reels."

Instagram Reels: Reels allow you to create short videos in your feed. The difference between a *reel* and a *story* is that you can save your Reels to your main Instagram feed, making them accessible forever. Remember that "stories" disappear after 24 hours. Reels, however, can be permanent.

According to Instagram's instructions, here is how to create a Reel:

"Select Reels at the bottom of the Instagram camera. You will see a variety of creative editing tools on the left side of your screen to help create your Reel, including:

- **Audio:** Search for a song from the Instagram music library. You can also use your own original audio by simply recording a Reel with it. When you share a Reel with original audio, your audio will be attributed to you, and if you have a public account, people can create Reels with your audio by selecting "Use Audio" from your Reel.
- **AR Effects:** Select one of the many effects in our effect gallery, created by Instagram and creators worldwide, to record multiple clips with different effects.
- **Timer and Countdown:** Set the timer to record any of your clips hands-free. Once you press record, you will see a 3-2-1 countdown before recording begins for the amount of time you selected.
- **Align:** Line up objects from your previous clip before recording your next to help create seamless transitions for moments like outfit changes or adding new friends to your Reel.
- **Speed:** Choose to speed up or slow down part of your selected video or audio. This can help you stay on a beat or make slow-motion videos.

Reels can be recorded in a series of clips (one at a time), all at once, or using video uploads from your gallery. Record the first clip by pressing and holding the capture button. As you record, you will see a progress indicator at the top of the screen. Stop recording to end each clip."

Instagram offers the following instruction for sharing Reels:

"With Reels, you can share with your followers, and they can be discovered by the vast, diverse Instagram community on Explore.

If you have a Public Account: *You can share your Reel to a dedicated space in Explore, where it has the chance to be seen and discovered by the wider Instagram community. You can also share your Reel* with your followers by posting it to your Feed. When you share Reels featuring certain songs, hashtags, or effects, your Reel may also appear on dedicated pages when someone clicks on that song, hashtag, or effect.

If you have a Private Account: *Reels follows your privacy settings on Instagram. You can share to Feed so only your followers can see your Reel. People will not be able to use original audio from your Reels, and people cannot share your Reels with others who do not follow you.*

Once your Reel is ready, move to the share screen, where you can save a draft of your Reel, change the cover image, add a caption and hashtags, and tag your friends. After you share your Reel, it will live on a separate Reels tab on your profile, where people can find the Reels you have shared. If you also share to your Feed, your Reel will appear on your primary profile grid, though you have the option to remove it.

Whether you have a public or private account, you can share your Reel to your Story, close friends or in a direct message. If you do so, your Reel will behave like a regular Story — it will not be shared to Reels in Explore, will not appear on your profile, and will disappear after 24 hours."

Finally, in addition to your regular *Feed, Stories,* and *Reels,* Instagram also offers a **Live** option and the recently added a **Live Room** feature, which allows you to live stream with up to three other people. Here are Instagram's instructions for Live Rooms:

"***Instagram Live:*** *To start a Live Room, swipe left and pick the Live camera option. Then, add a title and tap the Rooms icon to add your guests. You will see people who have requested to go live with you, and you can also search for a guest to add. When you start a Live Room, you will remain at the top of the screen when you add guests.*

As a broadcaster, you can add up to three guests at once or one by one (for example, you could start with two guests, and add a surprise guest as the third participant later). Going live with multiple guests is a great way to increase your reach, as guests' followers can also be notified."

Note that you do not have to do a "Live Room"; you can go live independently if you prefer. Regardless, the great thing about going live on Instagram is that you can now earn money from these videos. On May 27, 2020, Instagram announced the following:

"Creators have always been at the core of our community. Since the earliest days of Instagram, they have inspired people around the world with their talents, shared their lives, and built their personal brands from the ground up.

We have always been committed to supporting creators as they turn their passion into livelihoods; because every creator is unique, that means providing a mix of monetization tools to help creators of all sizes, from the emerging to the more established. Today we are announcing new ways for creators to make money through Instagram Live and IGTV.

Introducing Badges in Live: During the COVID-19 crisis, we have seen people supporting their favorite creators in Live with comments, likes, and donations. To give fans another way to participate and show their love, we are introducing badges that viewers can purchase during a live video.

In recent months, we have seen creators embrace Live in new ways, leading to a 70% increase in views from February to March. From fitness instructors to dancers, artists to chefs, Live has helped creators and businesses stay connected to their followers and bring people together. With badges, creators can generate income from the content they are already creating.

Badges will appear next to a person's name throughout the live video. Fans who have purchased badges in Live will stand out in the comments and unlock additional features, including placement on a creator's list of badge holders and access to a special heart."

Instagram Badges are available for viewers to purchase for 99 cents, $1.99, or three for $4.99. Essentially, they function like a "tip jar" for viewers to "tip" creators. Right now, *Badges* are only available to certain accounts; Instagram will notify you if you are eligible.

Of the three options - *Stories, Reels,* and *Live* - I only use *Stories.* To be honest, it is more important for me to get people to watch my YouTube videos because the payout is higher on YouTube versus Instagram. While some creators are making money with *Badges,* it is nowhere near what people are earning on YouTube, at least not yet. As long as you have ads enabled on your YouTube videos, you WILL earn a cut of AdSense revenue. However, there is no guarantee that anyone who watches one of your live Instagram videos will "tip" you.

However, it is still beneficial to learn all of the features a site offers, so definitely test out the *Reels* and *Live* Instagram options so you at least know how they work should you want to use them in the future. As they compete with other social media networks, Instagram is continually rolling out new features, so staying up to date with its offerings is important.

The best use of Instagram that I have found is to connect with subscribers on a more personal level. While I talk a lot about business on YouTube and Instagram, I share personal photos of my dogs, family, and life. I also post pictures of fun activities such as eating dinner out (Instagram users love food photos!) or attending local events. And I also post funny memes and jokes, which are always a hit and increase engagement.

Whatever my Instagram content, however, the main goal is to further connect with followers who are interested in the content I provide, whether it is on my YouTube channels or in the books I write.

Just like on Twitter, **hashtags** are a big part of getting your content on Instagram found. I like to include three to five hashtags with every photo I share. If I share a picture of a subscription box I have reviewed on YouTube, I might use hashtags such as:

- #subscriptionbox
- #unboxing
- #review
- #youtube
- #youtuber

TIP: You can create a long list of hashtags in the "notes" app on your phone and simply copy and paste them onto all of your Instagram posts. The goal of these hashtags is for the many Instagram users who search for specific hashtags to find yours, so using as many as possible increases your chances of being found. You can also put the hashtags in your Instagram *Stories*; however, I typically only add a couple because the hashtags take up space on the screen and can distract from the post itself.

Hashtags bring non-followers to my posts all the time. And not all of them end up following me. However, even if they do not follow me on Instagram, they may still check out my profile and click through to my Amazon Author Page or my YouTube channel. And again, driving traffic to the things I am earning money from is my ultimate goal.

When promoting my YouTube channel via Instagram, I post a thumbnail from my most recent video and encourage followers to head over to my channel to watch it. Since the link to my YouTube channel is in my Linktr.ee menu, which is linked in my bio, I usually write: *"New video now live on my YouTube channel; direct link in my profile @ann_marie_eckhart."* The "@" link will take users to my profile page, where the active link to my Linktr.ee menu, and therefore my YouTube channel, will be. Then the user simply clicks on my YouTube channel URL, taking them straight to my videos.

As with Twitter and Pinterest, it is a good idea to actively network with others on Instagram by following them back, "liking" their pictures and leaving comments. I like to spend about 10 minutes a day scrolling through my Instagram feed to check out what others are posting and engage with my favorite posts.

Note, also, that Instagram is an app. While you can see your Instagram feed, edit your profile, and add followers on a computer, you can only add your own posts using the app on your smartphone or tablet. Unlike Facebook and Twitter, which both work about the same on a cell phone or desktop computer, Instagram works best on mobile devices.

TIKTOK: TikTok is the new social media network on the scene, and it has taken off since it launched in 2018. In just a few short years, TikTok has amassed over 100 million users, making it arguably the fastest growing social media site online.

TikTok is an app-based, short-form video-sharing platform that allows users to create video clips anywhere from 15 seconds to three minutes long. Initially, TikTok was used mainly by those sharing music and dance; however, now, it is popular with nearly every demographic with a wide range of topics. From cooking and fashion to gossip and vlogging, TikTok now attracts celebrities alongside everyday folks who, even if they do not upload their content, love to scroll through the feed.

So how can you use TikTok to drive traffic to your YouTube channel? Any way you want to! It is up to you whether you want to pop on to let your followers know that a new video has gone live or want to share a clip of a recent video. Those who successfully utilize the site to grow their businesses post at least once a day on TikTok, so setting up a schedule will help you be consistent.

I like to share my recent Ebay sales on my TikTok feed. Not only does this drive traffic to my books, but it also gets people interested in my YouTube videos, as many of them are reseller related.

A great way to utilize TikTok is to create a post that you can share on Instagram, Facebook, and even YouTube. Here's how I do it:

In my TikTok account, I create a one-minute or less video of whatever it is I want to promote. Let's say it's my Etsy sticker shop. I often film short clips of new stickers and magnets that I've added to my shop.

Once my TikTok is live, I then download it to my phone. Next, I switch to Instagram and create a Reel with the clip. This is easy to do: I just click on "Reel" and upload the video clip from TikTok that I downloaded to my phone (it will be in my camera roll). After the Reel is life, I share it on my Stories.

I then go to Facebook and post the TikTok to my Facebook pages. I like to cross post my Etsy shop to my main @anneckhart Facebook page and the page for my shop, @jeanleepublishing.

Finally, I upload the TikTok clip to YouTube. If it is under 15 seconds, I can add it as a YouTube Short (more on Shorts coming up). If it is longer than 15 seconds, I will add it as a video upload to my channel the same way I do a full-length video. Using YouTube Studio, I will then copy and paste the text from the description box of a recent full-length video to the description box of the TikTok video. I can also monetize the video in YouTube Studio.

In under 10 minutes, I will have created a TikTok, Instagram Reel, Instagram Story, Facebook Post, and YouTube post with just ONE short video! That's what I mean when I talk about cross-promotion!

Just like Instagram, TikTok allows only one link in a creator's profile. If you want to put more links in, you can use one of the "link tree" landing page plug-ins that I laid out earlier. My link is linktr.ee/anneckhart. This one link opens up to show all of my links/

Fortunately, TikTok allows users to link their Instagram and YouTube channels in their bios and provides the icons for each site. This frees up your primary link to add in a link to your website or Facebook page. I personally have my Amazon Author Page as my link, and then I link Instagram and YouTube with TikTok's interface.

YOUTUBE SHORTS: In 2022, YouTube introduced **YouTube Shorts**, letting you create, edit and share short videos. YouTube Shorts are a direct result of TikTok's exploding popularity in the short-form video market. Longer videos are out, and short videos are in. And by short, we're talking 60-seconds or less.

Shorts are meant as a way to engage your subscribers further and also attract new viewers. They are easy to film and upload with your mobile device.

To create a Short, simply follow these steps:

1. Sign into the YouTube app on your mobile device
2. Tap the plus sign inside of the circle to Create a short
3. To make your Short longer than 15 seconds, tap 15 above the record button to record up to 60 seconds (if you add in music, the video is limited to 15 seconds)
4. Record your clip the same way you would record any video using your mobile device
5. You can undo and redo clips if you wish
6. Tap Done to preview and enhance your video
7. Save as draft
8. Tap NEXT to add details to your video. Add a title (maximum 100 characters) from this screen and choose the video settings. I like to select "private" and finish the Short on my laptop, but you can make it live from your device if you are ready.
9. Tap Select audience and choose Yes, it's made for kids or No, it's not made for kids
10. Tap UPLOAD. If you choose Public, your Short will go live. If you choose Private, your short will remain on Private until you edit it to Public.

Or you can use the TikTok method I talked about earlier and just upload a TikTok that is 60-second or less and that doesn't contain licensed music and turn it into a Short. I'm all about efficiency, so if you are already making TikTok's, turning them into YouTube Shorts is a quick and easy way to expand your reach.

Right now, you cannot earn AdSense money from Shorts. However, YouTube has invested $100 million into a Shorts Creator Fund to help build the feature.

YOUTUBE LIVE: Another interesting feature available to YouTube creators is YouTube Live, which enables you to go live on the platform. Whether you go live alone for a casual chat with viewers or host an event with other creators, YouTube Live is another way to engage with followers and attract new viewers.

You can live stream on YouTube with your webcam, mobile device, or encoder streaming. StreamYard is a popular program that makes going live on YouTube easy and with better picture quality than most webcams.

NETWORK WITH FELLOW YOUTUBERS: There is a fine line between networking with other YouTube creators to grow your channel and outright using them to help you. One of the most painful things I see new YouTubers do is BEGGING people to subscribe to their channel. They stalk successful YouTube channels and leave comments asking the viewers of someone else's channel to sub their channel. Or worse, they send out private messages to the subscribers of other channels asking them to subscribe.

If you are creating quality content, there is no reason to beg for subscribers. In fact, it is so tacky and frowned upon nowadays that you will likely turn off potential viewers. However, there are ways that you can network with other YouTube creators that are beneficial for both you and them.

First, you want to SUPPORT other channels. Subscribe to the channels you genuinely like, give their videos a thumbs up, leave nice comments, and share their videos via your social networks

(I like to share my favorite videos to both Twitter and Pinterest using the "share" buttons located under each video).

Showing your support to other channels not only helps your favorite YouTube creators, but it will likely get you noticed by their subscribers, drawing people to your channel. Again, do these things because you want to support channels you enjoy; you should help other creators without expecting them to return the favor, especially if the channels are much larger than yours.

Suppose you develop a friendly "relationship" with another YouTuber (they are replying to your comments or noticing your Tweets). In that case, it is okay to mention that you also casually make videos similar to theirs. But do so without expecting you will get anything back from them. Let these relationships develop naturally; just like in real life, genuine internet friendships are based on both parties having an equal amount of respect and admiration for one another.

Suppose you find another YouTube creator with the same number of subscribers as you have and who is creating similar content. In that case, you may want to suggest doing a collaboration video with them. Many YouTubers do "collabs," where they partner with another channel to create videos with similar themes.

Video collab ideas include sending each other boxes of goodies to open on camera, answering "tag" questions, or participating in group challenges. If you live in the same area, have gotten to know another creator well, and feel safe meeting them in person, you can even film videos together, posting a video to your respective channels and then directing viewers to go to the other channel to watch the other video. For instance, I have seen several resellers get together to shop at flea markets or antique malls. They each "vlog" their experiences and post them to their channels, encouraging their viewers to check out the other respective vlogs.

Collaboration videos help you make friends in the YouTube community; everyone benefits by encouraging viewers to check out all the participating channels. People who do collab videos link each other's channels in their video's description boxes, and the videos are then shared via everyone's respective social media accounts.

Create great content, support the channels you enjoy watching, utilize your social media accounts, and let the viewers and subscribers build naturally! After all, you want people to WATCH your videos, not just hit subscribe because they have been paid or guilted into doing so.

TOP 10 SOCIAL MEDIA PLATFORMS:

1. Facebook: 2.9 billion users and $85.96 billion in revenue
2. YouTube: 2.2 billion users and 28.8 billion in revenue
3. WhatsApp: 2 billion users and $5.5 billion in revenue
4. Instagram: 2 billion users and $24 billion in revenue
5. TikTok: 1 billion users and $11 billion in revenue
6. Snapchat: 534 million users and $1.06 billion in revenue
7. Pinterest: 444 million users and $575 million in revenue
8. Reddit: 430 million users and $289.9 million in revenue
9. LinkedIn: 250 million users and $12.4 billion in revenue
10. Twitter: 217 million users and $5.42 billion in revenue

CHAPTER EIGHT: BEST PRACTICES

Great equipment, top-notch film quality, and consistent marketing are not enough to gain viewers and subscribers on YouTube. Follow these best practices to ensure your YouTube career is a success.

PAYING FOR SUBSCRIBERS: One thing you absolutely do NOT want to do is pay for people to subscribe to your YouTube channel. There are online companies that, for a price, will get people (usually automated computer "robots" or "bots") to subscribe to your channel. However, VIEWS are what create AdSense revenue, not subscribers.

First, people who have been paid to subscribe to a channel will not actually watch the videos. Second, some sites track YouTube channel subscribers, views, and revenue and post the results online, so it is obvious when someone has paid for subscribers, as there will be a sudden massive spike in their numbers. It can actually hurt your channel if you have a large number of subscribers but a low number of video views in comparison.

Slow and steady wins the race on YouTube!

CHANNEL DESIGN: When you log into YouTube, you can select **Your Channel** (click on your profile picture in the top left-hand corner, and it is the first option in the drop-down menu) to edit the design of your channel's homepage via the **Customize Channel** icon. Once on the Channel customization page, there are three sections you can work on: Layout, Branding, and Basic Info.

Under the **Layout** tab, you can add a **Channel trailer for people who haven't yet subscribed to your channel.** This acts as a commercial or preview for anyone who comes to your channel but is not yet subscribed. You can also upload a **Featured video for returning subscribers** to give a special welcome back for your loyal viewers.

Under the **Branding** tab, you can change your **Profile picture**, which is the photo that appears not just on your channel page but also next to all of your videos and next to any comments you post on your videos or anyone else's. A Banner image appears across the top of your channel. You need to provide an image that measures 2048x1152 pixels and 6MB or less. There are a lot of free apps that can create these specialty images; I personally use a YouTube thumbnail app that offers multiple sizes for social media graphics.

Finally, you can add a **Video watermark** that will appear on your videos in the video player's right-hand corner. An image that measures 150x150 pixels is recommended. The image must be a PNG, GIF (no animations), BMP, or JPEG file that is 1MB or less. My watermark is my YouTube channel logo.

Under the **Basic info** tab, you can add all of the links to your social media accounts, along with a blog/website if you have one—first, the field of writing your channel's description under **About.**

My About section on my main "Ann Eckhart" channel currently reads: *Hi, and welcome to my channel! My name is Ann, and I am an author and entrepreneur based in Iowa. On this channel, I talk about my various home-based businesses, including self-publishing books on Amazon KDP, running an Etsy sticker shop, and reselling vintage* collectibles on Ebay and WhatNot. If you are interested in making money online from home and being your own boss, then this is the channel for you!

On my second channel, "Ann Eckhart Vlog," my *About* section currently reads: *Hi, my name is Ann, and welcome to my vlog channel! Some of you may know me from my main channel, Ann Eckhart, where I discuss my home-based businesses. However, this channel is for my vlog content. From shop-with-me trips and recipes to theme parks and pug dogs, this channel is just a fun outlet for me where I can take time away from running my numerous businesses!*

In both *About* sections, I also provide my business email address, although I specify that it is for business inquiries only, such as sponsorship and brand deal proposals. I had to include that warning to stop people from sending me personal emails; I was getting so many messages a day that it took away from my ability to get any work done. It is one of those "tough love" moves you will have to make as your YouTube channel grows.

In addition to my email, I include my P.O. Box address for both PR and viewer mail. Having a P.O. Box is another decision you will want to make if you plan to build your YouTube channel, as you do not want to give out your home address to your viewers. You can get a P.O. Box from your local Post Office or UPS Store. Note that the boxes at USP Stores are considerably more than the regular postal boxes. I currently pay around $100 a year for my USPS P.O. Box.

In the middle of the "About" page is the **Links** section. Here is where you can add all of your other links. I currently have the following URLs linked: my Amazon store (this is where I have my books and a list of reselling supplies and household favorites), Facebook page, Twitter account, Instagram page, Pinterest board, and second YouTube channel.

The last two sections of the page are **Links on banner**, where you can choose one of your links to appear on your channel's banner, and **Contact info**, where you can again provide your email address. Since my main channel focuses on unboxings and reviews, I like to have my email linked twice for easy contact with brands.

DESCRIPTION BOX: When you upload a video to YouTube, you need to create a title and put some information in the description box below each video. I will share what is in my description box in the next chapter of this book, "A Day in the Life." Your description box should give your viewers directions for what you want them to do, and the first thing should be the most important as it is the only one viewers will initially see unless they expand the view to reveal everything written in the box.

Some YouTubers ask viewers to give their videos a thumbs-up, leave a comment, and subscribe as the first things in their description boxes. Since I am trying to drive traffic to my books, I list my Amazon Author Page first. Under that, I have all the links to my social networking sites, a bit about me, and my disclaimer. If I end my video by directing people to my social networking sites, I tell them that all my links are listed in the description box below and that they must click on the down arrow to bring everything into view.

I keep the verbiage in the description box of my videos in a Word document to simply copy/paste the information whenever I upload a new video. Because viewers only see the first three lines of the description bar unless they click to expand it, it is vital to put your most crucial directive there. Make sure any websites you link have the complete URL addresses to be "live," i.e., so viewers can click on them and be taken directly to your site.

ENCOURAGING LIKES, COMMENTS, and SUBSCRIPTIONS: While it may seem logical that people who watch and enjoy your videos will give them a "thumbs up," leave comments, and subscribe to your channel, most viewers will not give you any feedback whatsoever. As I mentioned earlier, many people will find your videos through internet searches or YouTube, recommending them to them while watching another creator's channel. Most viewers do not even have YouTube accounts, so while they can watch videos via the app or on their computers, they cannot respond to your videos in any way.

For viewers with a YouTube account, however, you want to encourage interaction as much as possible. YouTube offers those with a YouTube account the ability to "like" (i.e., click on the little "thumbs up" icon) videos; "dislike" (i.e., click on the small "thumbs down" icon), leave a comment on videos; subscribe to channels; add videos to a "favorites" list; and share videos to their social media accounts.

Encouraging people to do any of the above helps to promote your videos as the friends and followers of those viewers will see their activity and possibly decide to subscribe to your channel, too. I often forget to give the videos I am watching a "thumbs up" and will only do so when the creator reminds me.

At the end of most of my videos, I will ask people to leave me any questions or comments they might have. I will also ask them to "give it a thumbs-up if they liked the video." Finally, I suggest they subscribe to more videos if they have not already done so.

Some YouTube creators ask for likes and subscribers at the beginning of their videos, and some even mention it in the middle. What you do is up to you; you can always play around with this to see what feels the most natural.

MONITORING COMMENTS: Having viewers leave comments on your videos is something every YouTuber appreciates...unless those comments are mean. While most comments on my videos are positive, a "hater" comes along and says something rude or nasty now and again.

The more views a video gets, the more likely it is that someone will eventually leave a negative comment on it. The large YouTube channels whose videos get millions of views have to deal with an enormous amount of hate or "trolls," some of it so bad that it has driven successful YouTubers off the site.

Some YouTuber creators do not monitor the comments left on their videos, believing that free speech protects those who leave comments and feeling that any comment, good or bad, is engagement that ultimately benefits their growth. While I am all for free speech, I believe it comes with consequences. And the result for someone leaving a negative comment on one of my videos is that I remove the comment and ban the person from my channel so that they cannot interact with me on YouTube in any way (either by giving a video a thumbs down, leaving me a comment, or sending me a message).

My YouTube channel is my personal space. I would not allow someone to come into my home and treat me poorly, so I would not let them be mean to me through YouTube. Other creators don't care what types of comments are left on their videos. Only you can decide what you are comfortable with.

While the "thumbs down" option still appear under videos, it is no longer active. In 2022, YouTube removed the ability for viewers to give videos a "thumbs down," although they have yet to remove the icon. I like the change, while other creators view any type of engagement, even negative ones, as positive. We're all still waiting to see what YouTube ultimately decides to do with the "thumbs down" image.

Negative comments hurt, but most people who leave comments are kind and supportive. I try my best to reply to anyone who leaves a comment on any of my videos, although I usually only do this for the first day or two after the video goes live. Even if I cannot leave a written reply, I try to give nice comments a "thumbs up" and click on the little heart icon next to their comment to let them know I saw their comment.

The YouTube Studio App makes acknowledging comments easy as you can simply tape the "thumbs up" and "heart" icons. Depending on your mobile device typing skills, it can be difficult to type out a reply on your phone.

While YouTube used to send a message to you every time a new comment was left on one of your videos, they no longer do this. You get a notification of activity on your videos whenever you log in (there will be a little red box next to the bell icon at the top of the page with the number of activities – likes, comments, shares, subscriptions – that are new). Still, it is much harder to find and reply to comments, especially on older videos.

I like to go to my **YouTube Studio** (click on your profile picture in the top right-hand corner of the page; it is the third selection in the drop-down menu). This takes me to my **Channel dashboard**, and on the left-hand side of the page are several options I can choose from, including **Comments**. Once I click on the comment icon (a speech bubble), I am brought to a dedicated page where comments are listed in chronological order, allowing me to see the most recent comments that have been left. It is easy for me to reply to or like the comments, delete any that are inappropriate, and check on those marked **Held for review** or **Likely spam**.

Often people will continue to leave comments on videos months or even years after they were first put up and responding to those can be nearly impossible unless you go to the dedicated Comments page so that you can see the most recent comments that have been left. Do your best to reply to comments, or at least acknowledge that you are reading all comments in your videos.

You want to continually let your audience know that you appreciate all their "likes" and comments. However, the most successful YouTube channels do eventually have to stop reading and replying to comments as it is too time-consuming. At most, I may get 50 comments on a video, but it is usually much less, so it is still manageable for me. It is a great goal to have a video eventually with so many viewers and comments that you cannot keep replying to them!

PRIVACY: When the internet first became available, people could hide anonymously behind their computers, posting whatever they wanted under screen names without anyone knowing who or where they were. However, social media, and especially YouTube, has changed that. Even if you decide to make videos that do not appear on the screen, you will still expose yourself to the world. Therefore, it is important to take the proper safety and security measures.

Keep the exact location of your home to yourself. I only say that I live in Iowa; I do not mention the precise city. I do not show the front of my house. I have a P.O. Box for mail, so I do not have to give out my home address. I do not announce if I am going on vacation, not only so that people do not know I am not home but also not know where I will be.

I am a small-time YouTuber, and these measures may seem extreme. However, I am most comfortable with the level of privacy I have cultivated. I would rather be safe than sorry. Once you have exposed the city you live in or shown the front of your house, that information is online forever. Be extra careful when you are filming and even talking so that you do not give away too much of your privacy.

SCHEDULE & CONSISTENCY: If you are on YouTube to make money and build your brand, you will want to keep a consistent schedule of uploading videos. Some people upload on a specific day of the week, while others aim for a set number of videos per week. I typically like to post on my vlog channel on Monday, Wednesday, and Friday. For my main channel, I will post on the days when I do not have a vlog on the second channel to avoid releasing two videos on the same day. I also try to post at the same time on both channels just to create consistency.

No matter what my posting plans are, I try to keep my viewers updated on my schedule. If viewers expect a video, but something has come up, and I cannot upload it, I will try to post an update. I can do this directly on YouTube by posting on the Community tab of my channel, which will show up in my subscriber's feed. And I can also post about the schedule change on Facebook, Twitter, and Instagram. Viewers will forgive an interruption in your upload schedule if you keep them informed.

Nothing is worse than subscribing to a new YouTube channel that promises frequent videos, only never to see them again. If you are going to be successful on YouTube, you MUST commit to it. You cannot upload a few videos, abandon your channel, and then wonder why you do not have any subscribers and are not making any money. Find a filming schedule that works for you and stick to it, at least when you are first starting out.

I recommend starting out with one or two weekly videos and building on that schedule if you want to. The biggest mistake I have seen new creators make is trying to start a daily vlogging channel only to get burned out and abandon their YouTube career altogether. You can always build on your posting schedule, but it is tough to cut back on it as once viewers expect videos on specific days and times, they become agitated if you take content away.

YouTube analytics and viewers prefer videos that are around 15 minutes in length. Unless you are filming a vlog-style video or doing a live question and answer session or hangout, anything longer than 15 minutes is usually too long for most people. However, putting up videos that are too short may not satisfy viewers. And if viewers do not watch your video, you will not earn any AdSense revenue.

But of course, every situation and viewer is different. I watch channels that put up 10-minute videos and others that produce videos that are over an hour. Again, sticking to your guns and creating the content that pleases you is the most important thing, regardless of video length. Remember that videos must be at least eight minutes long to insert the Mid-Roll Ad Breaks we discussed earlier in this book. To maximize your AdSense income, you will want to aim for videos at least eight minutes in length so you can insert those ads.

However, more important than the length of videos is their QUALITY. As we discussed early on in this book, you do not need expensive camera equipment or editing software to produce quality YouTube videos (again, I film and upload videos on an iPhone). Still, you want your videos to be clear, steady, and well-lit. Speak up so viewers can hear you. Be sure you have a nice backdrop while filming a sit-down video. Do your best to provide your viewers with the kind of quality video you enjoy watching.

Before you upload your video and make it live, watch it back first to ensure it looks and sounds nice. I would rather reshoot a video or skip it altogether than upload one that is of poor quality. When I upload my videos, I have them set to "Private" so I can review them on YouTube before making them public. And as my filming has gotten better over the years, I have deleted old videos that were not up to my standards and reshot others.

VIEWS VS. SUBSCRIBERS: Most people start on YouTube focused solely on gaining subscribers. And while your number of subscribers is important to your channel's overall growth and your brand, the number of views your videos get is more important.

As I mentioned earlier in this chapter, I have seen people so focused on gaining subscribers that they have PAID people to subscribe to their channels. However, just because someone subscribes to your channel does not mean they will watch your videos. You only earn AdSense revenue from people WATCHING your videos, so paying for subscribers is a huge waste of time and money.

Only when someone watches your monetized videos and sees or clicks on the ads will you earn any Google AdSense revenue. To attract viewers, you need to produce quality content. Not all subscribers will watch all your videos, and not all viewers will become subscribers. Suppose you have one of two videos that draw many viewers from internet searches or YouTube promoting them. In that case, you may make a lot of AdSense money from people just watching your videos, even if they do not end up subscribing.

However, if you are like me and are doing YouTube for both profit AND fun, you will consistently upload new videos. While I have a handful of videos with current views of over 100,000, as of this writing, most of my videos average about 3,000 views each within the first week, some a bit less and some a bit more. Of course, the longer my videos remain on YouTube, the more views they will get. Your videos will continue to earn AdSense money as long as people continue to watch them!

I focus on creating quality content that I am personally interested in, hoping that the viewers will respond. While I love earning AdSense, I never make a video, thinking it will make me money. I make videos that I enjoy filming and hope others will benefit from. Sometimes my favorite videos are the least viewed. However, I just continue making the videos I want to make, and eventually, like-minded people find them.

Making videos is time-consuming, so if I am not having fun, I will not do it. Viewers are smart and will see right through an attempt to film videos strictly done for views. Be yourself, have fun, and the views and subscribers will come!

DEALING WITH TROLLS: While most viewers who leave comments on YouTube videos are kind and encouraging, the longer you are on the site, the more likely it is you will encounter trolls, those negative people who will give your videos a thumbs-down just because they can and who hide behind fake names to leave nasty comments.

While it is tempting to fight back against mean commenters, I have found that ignoring them is the best thing to do. These people love to push buttons; they want creators to engage with them in hopes they can escalate the fight.

What do I do when someone leaves an inappropriate comment on one of my videos? I delete the comment and block the person from my channel. I do the same for anyone who leaves inappropriate comments on my other social media accounts.

My stance has always been that if I would not allow someone to speak to me a certain way in person, I certainly will not allow them to do it online. Especially when I do not even know who they are.

People online can be mean; they lash out because they are unhappy. As the saying goes, "Hurt people hurt people." And since YouTube allows users to hide behind screen names, it is easy for these types of viewers to leave negative comments.

If you are going to be on YouTube, you will have to develop a thick skin. Keep your focus on creating good content and connecting with the viewers who are kind; the bad ones are not worth your time. And, hey, at least they watched your video, and you earned AdSense from it!

THE TOP 25 MOST SUBSCRIBED TO YOUTUBE CHANNELS:

1. T-Series
2. YouTube Movies
3. Cocomelon
4. SET India
5. YouTube Music
6. PewDiePie
7. Gaming
8. Kids Diana Show
9. MrBeast
10. Like Nastya
11. WWE
12. Zee Music Company
13. Vlad and Niki
14. 5-Minute Crafts
15. YouTube Sports
16. BLACKPINK
17. Justin Bieber
18. Canal KondZilla

19. Goldmines
20. HYBE LABELS
21. BANGTANTV
22. Sony SAB
23. Zee TV
24. Shermaroo Filmi Gaane
25. Dude Perfect

CHAPTER NINE: A DAY IN THE LIFE

Being a YouTuber, even at a part-time or even hobby level, involves more than just filming and uploading videos. In this chapter, I will share a day in my life of everything I do to film, edit, upload, and release YouTube videos, including how I film both sit-down and vlog-style content.

And remember, I film, edit, and upload everything on my iPhone! Currently, I am using an iPhone 11.

First up, I will walk you through the process for uploading videos to my main channel, which is simply named "Ann Eckhart." I currently upload a new video on my main channel once or twice a week, depending on if I have anything actually to film. Since this channel focuses on my home-based businesses, I share updates of what I'm working on, new products in my Etsy shop, and previews of things I am listing on Ebay and WhatNot.

I like to film videos in advance as much as possible. I also like to space videos out between my two channels. In this example, I'm going to only upload one video this week on my main channel. I like to upload videos to my main channel on Sundays, so this gives me the entire week to film this week's one video.

For this example, I will film a casual, chatty video where I catch viewers up on my various businesses. I will set my tripod stand near my desk and angle my phone to get the best angle possible. This is difficult in my office, as I run several businesses out of one room. The space can look cluttered no matter how much I tidy up. But because my viewers are used to me being honest about what it takes to run home-based businesses, some stuff in the background isn't too bothersome.

I used to film sit-down videos with a table and chair set up in front of some bookcases in the corner of my office. I had neatly arranged books and items on the shelves behind me, and the setup was near a large window, which let in natural light.

Then I decided to move my entire reselling business (I sell vintage collectibles on Ebay and WhatNot) into my office, and the bookshelves were transformed into inventory storage. So, filming at my desk is my only option.

I gather everything I will need for the video, including anything I may want to unbox (viewer mail) or open (new Etsy sticker inventory) and scissors to open things up, my reading glasses or a magnifying glass to read small print, wet wipes to clean up any messes, lip balm to prevent my lips from drying out, and a bottle of water to keep my mouth hydrated.

Once everything is in place, and the camera is at the right angle, I press record and start filming. I have been making YouTube videos for over 12 years now and can usually film in one take, meaning I do not start and stop talking or filming. Occasionally, I will do a little editing of the footage; but I often only need to cut out the first and last seconds to come up with the final product.

After I have finished filming, I clean up and put everything away. I do this immediately so as not to get overwhelmed by the mess!

I then sit down with my iPhone and open **Settings**. Under **Display & Brightness**, I click on **Auto-Lock** and change the time to **Never**. Why? Because I want to make sure my screen does not go into sleep mode, which will stop the upload. This is an important step and one that I am embarrassed to admit that I often forget.

Next, I open the **iMovie app.** The app connects to my camera roll, and from here, I can add the video clip or clips into the app. I watch the video from beginning to end and make any cuts I feel are necessary. I then save the video by simply clicking **Save Video** within the app. iMovie saves the finished video back onto my camera roll.

Once the finished video is saved from iMovie to my camera roll, I **open the YouTube app on my phone** and make sure I am logged into my "Ann Eckhart" channel (remember, I have two channels; fortunately, the YouTube app makes it easy to alternate back and forth between the two with one click), and **click on the + sign inside of the circle** at the bottom of the page to begin the upload process.

I choose to **Upload a video**, which opens up my camera roll. From here, I select the video I just created in iMovie. I make sure that the **privacy setting is turned to "Private"** so that the video does not go live immediately (remember that I schedule my videos in advance; plus, I need to do some work on the back end before going live).

I then click **Upload** and wait for the video to be uploaded to my channel. How long this takes depends on the video's length and the speed of your internet or WIFI connection.

Once the video has successfully been uploaded, I **switch to my desktop computer to take care of the back-end details, which is much easier to do on my laptop than on** my phone. I log onto YouTube and go into my **YouTube studio**. I then click on the **Content** icon link on the left-hand side of the page and am taken to my channel videos list. The video I just uploaded should be the first video at the top of the page. I hover my mouse next to the video, revealing several icons. I click on the **pencil icon**, which is called **Details,** to access the **Video details** page.

Once on the video details page, I type in a **keyword-loaded title** so that people who are not subscribed to my channel might find it. I also try to make the title sound exciting to encourage people to watch it. There are so many videos on YouTube these days, making it highly competitive. You must be creative in getting people to click on your videos, especially when they first go live.

After the title, I go into a Word document I have on my computer and copy/paste a block of text that I put into the **description box**. For both of my channels, I link my Amazon store, where I have my books, reselling products, and household favorites listed. I also link my Etsy shop, my Ebay store, my WhatNot profile, and all of my social media sites.

I also include a **Disclaimer**: *This is not a sponsored video. If disclosed, some products were sent to me for review. Links may contain affiliates/referrals.*

The disclaimer is important per FTC rules. At the bottom of the page is a Paid Promotion section where you check a box to see if you received money for your video. If the video I uploaded had been sponsored, I would have also needed to disclose that in the description box and verbally state it in the video.

At the bottom of the description box, I add **three hashtags**, which YouTube will put at the top of the video when it goes live. This is a new YouTube feature, and it works to help people find similar videos through hashtags. For instance, if the video is a Halloween-themed Dollar Tree haul, I would use the hashtags *#dollartree #haul* and *#halloween.*

The **Tags** field is at the very bottom of the page. Here, you can add even more words (think of tags as hashtags without the # symbol) to help potential viewers find your videos when they do a YouTube search. I keep an extensive list of these tag words, separated by commas, in the same Word document where I have my description box information. I can simply copy and paste this block of words into the tags section of every video. I then click on the **SAVE** button before editing another section.

Next, I monetize my video by clicking on the **Monetization icon (the "$" symbol).** Clicking on that dollar icon brings me to the **Video monetization page.** At the top of the page is a **Monetization box**; I select **On** from the drop-down menu. This will allow me to access the option under the **Type of ads** section of the page. I check every box available: **Overlay ads, Sponsored cards, Skippable video ads,** and **Non-skippable video ads.** The **Display ads** option is automatically selected for you by YouTube.

At the bottom of this page is **Location of video ads.** If my video is over 10 minutes long, I can select all three options: **Before video (pre-roll), During video (mid-roll),** and **After video (post-roll).** Under the During video (mid-roll) option, click on **MANAGE MID-ROLLS**, which brings up a pop-up window titled **$ AD BREAKS.**

Here, I can choose where the ads that run in the middle of my videos will appear. These ads bring in the most AdSense revenue, so it is essential to make sure you place them strategically. Too many ads can turn viewers off, but not enough can negatively affect your AdSense earnings. I generally like to place ads around the six to the eight-minute mark of each of my videos, although for really long videos (over thirty minutes), I will use less so as not to turn off viewers with too many ads.

On the **$ Ad breaks page**, you can click on **+ AD BREAK** to add in however many ads you want to appear. Let us say that the video I am working on is 20 minutes long. I will likely add in two ad breaks. I will then move over to the **PLACE AUTOMATICALLY** column to enter in the times of six and twelve minutes, or around thereof. Note that you can also manually place the ads using the scrolling template at the bottom of the page, but I find it easier just to enter the times. Once I am done placing my ads, I click on the **CONTINUE** icon to be taken back to the Video monetization page.

After I have typed in my title, copied and pasted in my description and tags, and set up my video's monetization, I go back to the main **Video detail page (the pencil icon titled "Details")**. Until now, I have been using the links on the left side of the page to edit my video's information. Now I will focus on the right side of the page and the options that appear there.

I like to schedule my videos, and I do this under the **Visibility** section. When I uploaded my video from my iPhone to YouTube, I ensured it was set to "Private." Now I can change that from **Private to Unlisted, Members Only, Public (set as instant Premiere)**, or **Schedule**. I click on the **Schedule** option, which creates a new window of possibilities. I schedule my video for 2 pm Central time on Sunday, meaning it will stay private until YouTube publishes it at that time.

Note that I could also choose the **Set as Premiere** option so my subscribers would see a live countdown before the video goes live. Premiere also features a live chat option where viewers can chat with one another while the video plays. Some creators schedule premieres to be in the chat once the video goes live to talk with their viewers.

Premieres are a great way to encourage engagement with your viewers by providing you with a way to connect with them directly. Chatting with your viewers when your videos go live does help increase engagement and create more loyal subscribers, so it is something to consider doing, at least occasionally.

Once I have scheduled my video, I click on **DONE,** and the pop-up window collapses. Note that you do not have to schedule your videos to go up at any particular time; you could make them live once you have added your title and description and set up the video's monetization.

However, the YouTube algorithm seems to favor channels where the videos go up on set days at set times. And if you like to film videos ahead of time, scheduling them will help keep you organized. Many YouTube creators will film several videos on the same day and schedule them to go live over the following days or weeks.

The following section you can attend is **Playlists**. Playlists allow you to set up categories for your videos. For instance, I have playlists for Ebay videos, subscription boxes, vacation vlogs, and shopping hauls. If you create different types of videos, even if they are under the same general theme, you may want to consider creating playlists. When someone watches a video in a playlist, it will automatically play the next video in the line-up. Therefore, playlists help keep viewers on your channel and watching your videos.

The next section is the **End Screens**. Here you can add **Elements** to the end of your video that viewers can click on. You can add links to the following: **Video, Playlist, Subscribe, Channel, Link,** and **Merchandise**.

Adding a **Video element** lets you choose from **Most recent upload, Best for viewer,** or **Choose specific video.** I typically select the "Best for viewer option," but you can decide what is best for each video. For instance, if you referenced another of your videos in your uploaded video, you could select that one.

If you have created **Playlists** on your channel, you can also choose to add one of those to your video. **Subscribe** is another option, and along with "Video," Subscribe is my favorite option to add. **Channel** allows you to add another channel; I use it to promote my second channel. **Link** lets you add a clickable link to a URL that takes the viewer off YouTube and another site. And finally, **Merchandise** will take viewers to items you have created using the TeeSpring design feature that YouTube offers to channels with 10,000 or more subscribers. I have created merchandise using YouTube's TeeSpring feature and on the off-site platform TeePublic.

I typically only choose the "Video" and "Subscribe" elements for my videos; getting viewers to watch another video on my channel and having them subscribe are the two most important things I would like them to do. You want to be careful of loading too many end screen elements as your screen will look too cluttered to viewers, and they likely will not choose any of the options available.

The last box you can open is **Cards**, which, according to YouTube, "are designed to complement videos and enhance the viewer experience with relevant info." Cards help to point viewers to your other videos and off-YouTube content. You have four types of **Cards** to choose from: **Video, Playlist, Channel,** and **Link**.

Video cards allow you to link to another public YouTube video that viewers might be interested in. **Playlist cards** let you connect to another public YouTube playlist. **Channel cards** will enable you to link to a channel you want to direct viewers to; for example, maybe you are doing a collaboration video with another creator, so you create a "Channel card" to link them directly. And finally, **Link cards** allow you to link to **Associate website cards, Crowdfunding cards,** and **Merchandise cards**.

I do not use the "Card" options, feeling that the "End screen" options provide the same benefits. However, as you continue with your YouTube journey, you can take time to play around with the "Card" features to see if they work for you.

My title, description, tags, monetization, schedule, playlist, and end screen options are all finished. I am now ready to tackle the final task before my video is ready to launch: the **thumbnail**. A YouTube thumbnail is the image that appears next to the title of your video. It is the first thing a potential viewer sees, and it is imperative to help get people to click on your video and watch it.

You can use several design apps and programs to create correctly sized YouTube thumbnails. I use the **Thumbnail Maker app**, which is available from Apple and on Android devices. YouTube thumbnails need to be 1280x720 pixels; be uploaded in JPG, GIF, or PNG format; and remain under the 2MB limit.

To create my thumbnails, I first select an image. Sometimes I will use a photo, other times graphics, and in some cases, I will use both. I typically take a screenshot from my video and use that, adding text with the app. Using an app such as Thumbnail Maker makes it extremely easy to create my thumbnails right on my phone.

And once I save the finished product, I can add it to my video using the **YouTube studio app** on my phone to upload it directly to my channel.

At that point, my video is complete and ready for YouTube to make it live at the scheduled time!

I also have a vlog channel, *Ann Eckhart Vlogs*, but the process of uploading videos to that channel is relatively the same as it is on my main channel. The only difference is in the filming. While I focus on sit-down videos for my main channel, when I am filming a vlog, I am either filming myself or the events around me but not from a sitting position.

When filming video clips using my phone, I make sure to hold them horizontally, not vertically. Filming on an iPhone held vertically will result in black bars appearing on either side of your footage. Filming horizontally makes it so that your footage takes up the entire screen.

When vlogging, I simply film various video clips, which are automatically saved to my phone's camera. When I am ready to put all of the clips together, I do the same as I did for uploading my main channel video using my iPhone:

- I put all the clips together in iMovie
- I save the finished video to my camera roll
- I make sure to turn the sleep mode off on my phone so that my camera will not switch off during the uploading process
- I open the YouTube app and click on the "upload video" + sign in a circle icon at the bottom of the page
- I choose the video from my camera roll

- I click upload
- Once the video is uploaded, I switch over to my computer
- I add in my title, fill out the description box, add in my three leading hashtags, copy/paste my list of tags, monetize the video, choose a playlist, add my end cards, and finally, schedule the time and date I want the video to go live

Once my videos go live, I share them on my social media accounts. I use the **Share icons** located underneath my videos to post them to my Facebook page, Twitter account, and Pinterest board. I also put up a post on Instagram, both on my page's feed and in my "stories."

When I had my blog, I would also post my video there. And while theoretically, I could also post a short "commercial" for my video on TikTok. However, that would involve basically filming an entirely new video. I've yet to see TikTok users follow creators over to YouTube, so it isn't something I'm currently doing.

And that is it! That is the entire process I go through to film, edit and upload YouTube videos. I am sure that if you have never done it before, it can seem overwhelming. But trust me when I tell you that it will become second nature after you have uploaded a few videos of your own.

The other work I do concerning YouTube is answering emails from companies who reach out with sponsorship or product offers. Of course, driving is often a part of my vlog videos, so I need to track my miles and any money I spend on my channel.

I do YouTube for three reasons:

1. It is fun. I like to engage with viewers and have met good friends through the platform.
2. It is great advertising for all of my businesses.
3. The money. I don't make the amount of AdSense I used to, but I usually earn enough every month to pay for

my car!

CONCLUSION

With just a camera or smartphone and a computer, anyone can start a YouTube channel. However, it takes commitment and perseverance to make MONEY on the site. While a handful of people have gotten rich over the years by making videos, for most people, YouTube offers a bit of extra spending money, perhaps even enough to qualify it as a part-time job. How much you earn is up to you regarding how much time and effort you are willing to put into producing quality content that viewers respond to.

Putting yourself out there in front of thousands and potentially millions of people is a scary proposition. However, if you approach YouTube for your own personal enjoyment and growth before anything else, you will have a successful channel that also brings you some income.

YouTube can be stressful. Dealing with negative comments, having to redo videos, and navigating through technical difficulties can all take their toll. The good thing is that your YouTube channel is YOURS. You can put up as many videos as you want or as few as you want. Need a break? Take it! Step away for a few days, a week, or even a month. Yes, consistency is rewarded on YouTube, but not at the expense of your mental health.

Start your YouTube channel for fun. And at the beginning, just focus on having fun with your channel. There is no need to worry about the social media stuff and back-end work. Just get some videos up to get your feet wet. No one likes the first videos they film, and that is okay. Not looking into the camera, realizing you have a stain on your shirt, mispronouncing words....it all comes with the territory.

Practice really does make perfect when it comes to running a YouTube channel. Trust me that the more videos you film, the more comfortable you will become. You will find your footing and your voice. And you will find your audience. Trust me that there are people out there just wanting for the type of content you will produce. With consistency, they will find you.

There will be times you want to quit, but I urge you to just stick with it. It can be hard in the beginning when you aren't yet monetized, but once you hit 1,000 subscribers and have 4,000 watch hours, you will start to earn money on your videos. And being paid for your work is even more rewarding.

With all the work involved, why do I make YouTube videos? After all, it's not a full-time job for me. I've had many ups and downs on the site. I've cried over mean comments. I've been jealous when other creators blew past me with their subscriber counts. And I've been so discouraged that I just wanted to delete every video I ever filmed.

But no matter how frustrated I've gotten with YouTube over the years, I always return to the platform. After all, most of my online "friends" are fellow creators. I have a small community of like-minded entrepreneurs on the site who always have my back no matter what I do.

At the end of the day, YouTube is just plain FUN! I've filmed everything from baking videos to Walt Disney World vacation vlogs. I've gotten tons of free products from brands. I have videos of the days I brought my two dogs home. I have thousands of hours of professional and personal footage of my life that I can look back on at any time.

And the money can be good. Whether it is from Google AdSense directly or from the sale of my products, YouTube has been a huge part of my business success. I don't think I would have sold near the number of books I have over the years had my YouTube viewers not been the first ones to buy them. My subscribers have also been my first Etsy customers, and they now come to my live WhatNot auctions to buy the vintage collectibles I resell.

YouTube is now woven into my daily life. Even on days when I'm not filming or uploading, I'm still checking my channels and replying to comments. The customer base I've cultivated on YouTube is a big part of my self-employment success. I can't imagine giving it up!

And as for YOU: If you haven't already started a YouTube channel, I hope this book has inspired you to take the leap. And if you already have a channel but are struggling, just know I've been there, too. YouTube is, after all, a business. It's a job. Jobs can be fun. But they can also be hard.

But with YouTube, YOU are your own boss. You set your own hours and your own rules. Stay true to yourself and create the content you are passionate about. The views, the subscribers, and the money will come in time. But more importantly, you will gain confidence in having built up something that is uniquely yours!

◆ ◆ ◆

If you have a YouTube channel or create one after reading this book, please email me at seeannsave@gmail.com so I can check it out and subscribe!

One last thing: If you enjoyed this book, I'd appreciate it if you took a moment to leave a review for it on Amazon. Reviews are crucial in helping me to sell my books. Thank you!

Are you interested in other ways you can make money online? Be sure to visit my **Amazon author page at https://amzn.to/3wBF0WF** for all of my business books and planners, including:

- **Beginner's Guide To Amazon KDP: 2023 Edition**
- **Beginner's Guide to Selling On Ebay: 2023 Edition**
- **101 Items To Sell On Ebay**
- **101 MORE Items To Sell On Ebay**
- **2023 Reselling Planner & Accounting Ledger**
- **2023 Ebay Reselling Planner & Accounting Ledger**
- **2023 Postmark Reselling Planner & Accounting Ledger**
- **2023 WhatNot Reselling Planner & Accounting Ledger**
- **2023 Etsy Vintage Reselling Planner & Accounting Ledger**
- **2023 Etsy Sticker Shop Planner & Accounting Ledger**
- **2023 YouTube Channel Planner & Accounting Ledger**
- **2023 Amazon KDP Author Planner & Accounting Ledger**
- **2023 Amazon KDP Low Content Planner & Accounting Ledger**

ABOUT THE AUTHOR

Ann Eckhart is a writer, entrepreneur, and online content creator based in Iowa. She has numerous books available about how to make money online from home. For all of her books, visit her Amazon Author Page at: https://amzn.to/3wBF0WF

◆ ◆ ◆

You can also follow Ann Eckhart on these social media sites:

FACEBOOK: https://www.facebook.com/anneckhart/

TWITTER: https://twitter.com/ann_eckhart

INSTAGRAM: https://instagram.com/ann_marie_eckhart

MAIN YOUTUBE CHANNEL: https://tinyurl.com/yxvqtwc7

YOUTUBE VLOG CHANNEL: https://tinyurl.com/mvx84bfw

COPYRIGHT 2022 Ann Eckhart

No part of this book may be reprinted or reproduced without express written permission from the author.

Cover Design by Ann Eckhart

Made in the USA
Las Vegas, NV
06 December 2023